Adopted Instead

Lives Touched Because I Lived

By

James D Tranchina

Dedication

I am dedicating this story to all of my brothers and sisters whose life ended before it began. A special thanks to my cousin Frances without whose encouragement and help this would not be possible.

TABLE OF CONTENTS

Introduction

I am an adoptee born in 1951. The shocking circumstances surrounding my birth would not be clear to me until 1998. During this troubling 47-year period, I experienced many adventures and tribulations with my adoptive parents, multiple "surrogate" fathers who followed and finally with my birth mother and family. I often asked myself: 'what if my life had been aborted due to the circumstances surrounding my birth? What if my life had never occurred?'

Join me on my journey through these uncertain times filled with chaos and confusion as I explore my life experiences in this collection of stories. Don't be concerned for me though, because despite the circumstances, my life was and is filled with much wonder and miracles.

Many Homes for an Unwanted Child

Soon after my birth at Camp Pendleton, USMC, in Oceanside, California I was sent to San Diego for placement in a Catholic run orphanage. During my short stay with the Nuns, I was farmed out to foster parents. Fortunately, I have few recollections of that period.

I apparently spent some time with a Navy family based on my frequent reference to sailor hats, as "Petie" hats. Later, my adoptive parents would contact the orphanage to find out if there had been a Pete in my past. The answer was yes!

The only other significant memory during this time was related to an incident with a foster family's own daughters who used me as a play doll to put on make-up and dress me like a little girl. Somehow this had a major impact on me and I still remember the disdain I felt at the time.

Finally, a Forever Home

Finally, in 1954 at age 3 ½ years old, I met a woman named Josephine (Jo) and her husband Dennis. They would eventually adopt and give me a home. My first memory as someone's child were the first words my new Mother said when she informed me that she had gone to the orphanage to look for a little girl. After she saw me she said she changed her mind and only wanted me. This memory haunted me in the years that followed. This memory was one of many occurrences in my early years that would impact my self-esteem throughout life.

Being an orphan isn't the same as a normal child born into a real family. My tender age, however, didn't preclude me from learning some very harsh facts about life. For example, I remember being afraid to close my eyes at night for fear I might lose my few possessions, or worse and I even remember sleeping under my bed. I began to cultivate the foundation of my life's philosophy shortly after I was adopted.

Not long after my new parents took me home I remember the first of many times I would be introduced to a stranger. I heard these hurtful words so many times in the coming years that I started to shun situations where I might be introduced. Every time I met a new person this is how I was introduced: "this is Jim...we adopted him". That was often followed by the question: "Is he a Bastard (or something equivalent)?"

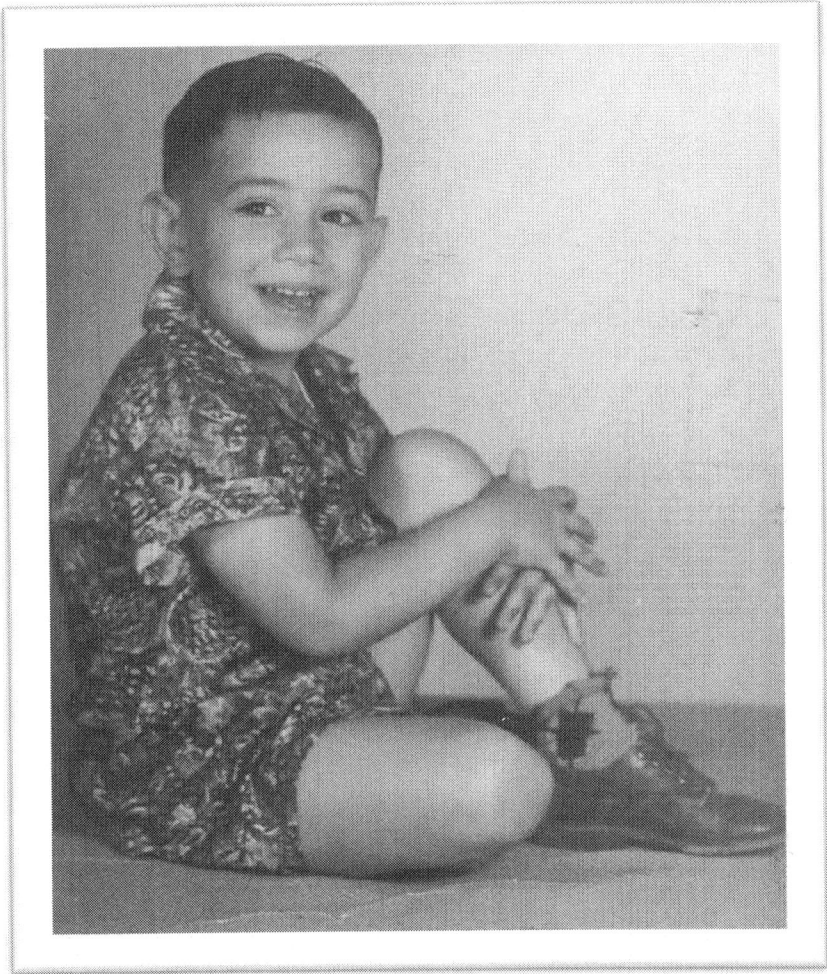

It would be some years before I understood what people were seeking when they asked that question. I suppose the silver lining here is that for a few years I was spared the shame of knowing and the blow to my self-esteem. Eventually I learned the harsh meaning and that triggered thoughts about how I had come to be.

Fortunately for me, my adoptive mother Josephine, (or Jo as she preferred), was always willing to let me seek out my biological parents. Many years later I discovered that for which I had spent a lifetime searching. Somehow when the revelation came, it broke a fragile bond between us that had been tested many times before and I lost all contact with Jo.

My search would be completed the day I met with my biological Mother—the woman who brought me into this world; even though my success sacrificed my relationship with Jo. I realized that her ego was too fragile to accept the process of my searching, and ultimately finding my birth Mother.

My 3 Rules of Survival

By the time I was 20, I had a total of two Mothers and five Fathers. You could infer that I was very hard on parents although it was never a conscious effort on my part. In fact, I always tried to be perfect, undoubtedly out of a feeling of debt to my adoptive parents.

Because of my early experiences with multiple parents (foster, adopted or otherwise), my primary approach to life developed...SURVIVAL!

Rule #1: I believed that each person must provide for their own and always be prepared for any and all outcomes. This philosophy helped me to function quite well until I reached my 30's then slowly my life began to unravel. (This aspect of my odyssey will be discussed much later.)

Rule #2: Equally important as my first rule of survival was my belief that one should never stay in one place any longer than necessary. I undoubtedly developed this attitude because my parents were themselves nomadic. Until the age of 16, I didn't live at the same address for more than a 12-month duration. (Avoiding roots has its benefits but I would eventually learn its true value.) Living as a nomad means never having to commit to anyone or anything. You blow into town; make new friends and experience new situations; then leave before any problems or commitments present themselves.

Rule #3: I developed a hero fixation. Because I had such bad luck with fathers, I was forced to look elsewhere (for my father figure). I studied famous heroes who strongly influenced my approach to life with a sense of certainty. At the time, I felt that following their philosophy was the right path for me. One of those heroes was Alexander the Great. I marveled at what he accomplished by the time he was 19 years old. The others were Marco Polo and Homer.

The common thread among these men was all three made significant contributions and each had a degree of wonder-lust in their souls. Their examples helped me to develop my natural instincts and intuition which would form the basis of my life's philosophy.

Eventually, these survival tools would fail me, but at least for a time they kept me alive and breathing air.

My Daily Credo:
1. Be Good
2. Be Polite (at all times)
3. Be Productive
4. Be Direct
5. Keep it Simple

Meet My Adoptive Parents

Get ready now for a taste of chaos as I embark on a new life with my adoptive parents. It took some time before I could grasp the reality of having "real" parents, since I had no idea what that experience was supposed to be like.

Jo and Dennis probably fit the typical stereotype of a couple in the 1950's. She and her large Italian family were from New Orleans. I don't know much about his background because Dennis disappeared out of my life less than one year later. I do know that at the time he worked for an aeronautical firm in San Diego, California. They were both people of small stature and from all accounts I heard a cute couple in the view of the public.

Jo came from a family of three boys and two girls. Another sister died at a very early age. Jo's mother passed away when she was 12 years old. Eventually her father, Dominic would remarry one of his first wife's sisters who assumed the role of surrogate Mother.

As I stated, Dennis was a small man and I believe probably suffered from a Napoleon complex, which might help explain his alcoholism. He wouldn't be my only brush with the effects of alcohol abuse. Before the first year with my adoptive parents ended, I had many encounters with the "Demon Rum" and all the abuse that comes from that black hole of human existence.

One night after dinner I eagerly tried to help my Mother with the dinner dishes and accidentally broke a plate while trying to dry it. My memory fails me whether

Dennis was under the influence at the time but with his history it was very likely. He became so angry that he took me outside and broke apart an old orange crate in his uncontrolled fury, he proceeded to beat me and teach me a lesson. He did!

Amidst his tirade of both verbal and physical abuse against me, my new Mother had to take me to the local hospital for treatment. This abusive incident proved to be the "death nail" of their marriage union and Jo immediately started the Divorce process. She didn't stay divorced long, however, as she was remarried by the time I was 5 years old.

Many years later, while serving in the Air Force, I was in San Diego and located Dennis. Legally he was still my Father. During this one meeting, I realized what a small man he was in all aspects of his manhood. All things considered, the loss of Dennis was certainly a positive in my life. I don't believe I would have survived into my teen years, for I think he would have killed me at some point during one of his drunken rages. Unfortunately, my relationship with Dennis caused me to believe that no one could ever be trusted if I wanted to survive in this world (at least that's what I believed.)

Decades later, I learned that Dennis had remarried and had another child in this marriage, so somewhere out there in the world I have a legal half-sister that I have never met. Decades later I learned that I have another sister and a brother living in this world. Regretfully, I have never met either one nor do I believe they even know I exist.

Tormenting Thoughts Begin

By the tender age of 4, I had already lost my biological parents and an adoptive parent. My history of loss started a cycle of tormented thinking that almost drove me to suicide. I lived each day of my life with compelling questions about why I wasn't wanted at birth by my biological parents and why I lost the first real Father that I had ever known.

My young mind began to reason that surely, I must be in this situation because I did something to deserve what's happening. How could I possibly have value as a human being if no one wants me?

I was learning not to trust relationships because they can end in a heartbeat without warning. What I didn't understand about the loss of trust was that I was learning not to trust myself. Like many children, I felt that all things wrong in my world must be my fault. (I've always had the tendency to take responsibility for everything - good or bad.)

Another New Father and Grandparents
By the time I was 5 years old my Mother found her next spouse. Once again, I found myself in a new and foreign situation in terms of relationships. All of this was extremely confusing and stressful for a young boy; however, this relationship would be a good time in my life. (It would be at least another decade before I began to understand and appreciate why Jo moved from one man to another with little time between transitions.)

My new father, Herb, came equipped with a complete set of Grandparents for me. It didn't take long for me to find the hidden value of having Grandparents, Walt and Ann, in my life. They were ready to have a grandchild on which to shower attention and affection...and I was ready to receive it.

Herb would be one of the greatest influences in my life. Today I would say most of my external persona was modeled from the template of this man. He was a very jovial type and would teach me about humor; which in turn became one of my greatest assets and tools for survival and success in life.

Walt was a bombardier in WWII in the European theater and by the time I came into his life, he was retired from the real estate business. He would spellbind me with his stories of the war and the importance of service to my country. Ann was a sweet, caring and gentle lady who had been married once before. She had two sons from that marriage.

I also acquired an Uncle in this transaction; his name

was Donald. He was a true example of a party animal. He was a paraplegic due to an automobile accident some years earlier. While stationed in Las Vegas as a member of the USAF and following a night of revelry, he was involved in the accident that left him paralyzed over the right side of his body. As a result, Donald would spend the rest of his life permanently disabled and receiving a monthly government check. This income allowed him the freedom to live life on his own terms and he lived it to the maximum. Most of his time was spent hanging out with the actor, Victor Mature and partying at their local watering hole in Del Mar, California.

Deadly Conflict by My Father

One thing I found strange about my new family was that Herb and Donald seemed to be as different as day and night, even though they had been raised by the same people. Walt always seemed to have problems with his oldest step-son, Herb, and their relationship always seemed strained. Soon, that relationship would be strained to the breaking point. (It would be many years later, as a young man, before I fully realized what caused the ultimate failure in the relationship.)

When I was in my early 30's while working at the Nevada test site, I received a phone call explaining that my Uncle Donald had died and I was needed to be a pall bearer at the funeral. Losing my Uncle was bad enough but I was shocked to learn that Herb killed him. Yes! Herb took the life of my Uncle Donald in a Psychotic break while taking Antabuse and drinking alcohol. The combination triggered his break with reality and he stabbed Donald to death.

Afterward, Herb attempted to gas himself to death by sticking his head in the oven. Unfortunately, Walt and Ann lived next store and it was Walt who found the carnage and saved Herb's life. He could never forgive what he had done.

What troubled me during the services was hearing my Uncles' friends keep asking: "who is the pall bearer who looks just like Donald?" Apparently, I looked a lot like my Uncle. The stares from the crowd made me very uncomfortable.

Years later when Herb was released from a hospital for the criminally insane, he asked me to take responsibility for his custody, but I refused. After serving five years, Herb was released and subsequently returned to school where he earned a Master's degree in Psychology. Ironically, he became an Alcohol Counselor.

Is This the Start of a Normal Childhood?

Life was starting to fall into some semblance of normal for me but I suppose that should have been an indicator that I was about to get hit with additional traumas. Just as I was getting comfortable in my new family I found myself in the hospital with a set of inflamed tonsils. Granted, there were parts of the process that I didn't care for; like the pain, but this wasn't the experience it should have been. Instead, I found it to be quite enjoyable simply because I could eat all the popsicles I could handle. Perhaps this one event was responsible for why I ended up working my entire adult life as a Registered Nurse. I certainly enjoyed all the attention I received. I started to feel like maybe I did have some value.

Andy Warhol once stated that each of us has 15 minutes of fame. My first minute of fame began the first day in school at age 6. Herb and Jo both had just started new jobs at a restaurant in Oceanside, California. (I was intrigued by the location because it was close to my birthplace. I knew my biological parents had lived in Oceanside and that I had been born nearby at Camp Pendleton.)

Just before school started, Jo researched and learned that we lived only nine tenths of a mile from the school; therefore, I wouldn't be allowed to ride the school bus to school. Jo and Herb didn't seem concerned and told me that I could walk to school like they did when they were kids.

On the first day of school, Jo packed my lunch and sent me on my way, because they both had to go to work that morning. They gave me instructions to walk into the school office, find an adult and inform them that I was there to start school. I was assured that all would be taken care of by the school staff.

When I arrived, I found an administrative office filled with parents attempting to enroll their children in class. It struck me as weird that I was the only kid present who didn't have a parent with him. Finally, I got up the nerve and walked to the main desk. I found a very pleasant lady who inquired what I needed. I told her that I was here to attend school and that this was my first day. I'm sure she must have thought I was some kind of lunatic thinking I could start school on my own.

The Principal heard about my situation and took over my case himself. It must have been a slow news day for the local newspaper because they sent a reporter to cover the first day of school. This is where I got my first minute of fame.

The next thing I know I am standing in front of a cameraman taking my photo standing next the principal. That picture ended up on the front page of the newspaper that night with the corresponding story about a young man who wanted an education so bad that he was enrolling himself on his own.

Herb went out that evening and bought every copy of the paper he could find. Jo and Herb took all the credit for what had occurred as though they were celebrities. Frankly, I never understood what all the commotion was about. I was being raised by Jo to be responsible and to conduct myself as a well behaved young man. I had simply done as I was told to do. Why was everyone making such a fuss? I learned independence from this experience and would carry that lesson throughout the rest of my life.

Ironically, I always hated school; it was way too slow. Teachers never held my attention for long. I was a very poor student but I wasn't stupid. I learned early on to play the game and if I didn't make waves, I could glide through life without being noticed (unless I choose to be noticed).

Home Alone and Learning

Jo and Herb spent most of their time at work and I was left alone most of the time. Generally, I only interacted with them on the days they were off. Every day they left me a list of chores. When I returned home from school, (to an empty house) I did my chores, put a little effort into my homework and then watched TV. This was a typical routine for me.

By the time I was 8, I had been trained to function as an independent adult. I could cook, sew, iron, clean house and care for myself. I was maturing at such a fast pace that other people trusted me to baby-sit their children, even as an 8-year-old boy. It was my first experience as a worker.

Before I was 9, I had my first real job, as a dishwasher in a restaurant. Now at age 56, I can take pride in the fact I have held a job for 47 years. No doubt my early childhood experiences contributed to my work ethic. To wit, I have had over 100 jobs in my lifetime.

On the Move

Now before we continue I'd like to re-cap the parental score at this point. So far, I've had two mothers, and three fathers in my short life and the future didn't look bright for keeping the score down.

School would prove to be an on-going challenge mainly because we were always moving. I attended second grade at a school in Desert Hot Springs, CA because my parents were offered a job running a spa and restaurant in this small desert community. So, before I could plant roots and become comfortable, we were on the road moving again.

I spent one year at the local public school before I was transferred across the valley to a Catholic school in Palm Springs. This would be a significant time in my early years of development. I would experience the wonder of attending school for the first time without any indoctrination of the religious practices of the Catholic Church (More on this later.)

Desert Hot Springs is where I would start my first real paying job in a restaurant. Jo had to work during this time and the term "latch key kid" hadn't been invented yet, but that's what I was. I spent many hours at home alone until Jo finally decided to bring me to work with her where I'd hang out in the kitchen area. Fortunately, the boss wasn't the type of man to let a kid just sit around and do nothing. He put me to work washing dishes with the promise I could eat all the garlic bread that came back from the tables. This doesn't seem like much pay for work, but as a hungry kid, I thought I was in Heaven. I loved the garlic bread and enjoyed washing dishes. (Ironically, later in life I quit a dishwasher job in less than one hour.)

The boss had other ideas for me though. He began to teach me how to cook, food preparation and presentation. That lesson paid off some years later when I worked in our family owned restaurant. This would be one of the best jobs I ever held. (It must have been the bread!)

School and my First Religious Experience

My first day of school in the second grade would prove to be every bit the challenge I had grown used to by this time. My adoptive mother was born Catholic, but in my early years chose to follow the Jehovah Witness religion. This choice in no way prepared me for my first day in a Catholic school. I still remember that day as though it happened yesterday.

The Head Nun took all the kids into the church first thing that morning. She directed the boys to sit on one side and the girls on the other. We sat and waited a while for something but I didn't know what or why. I noticed a boy on the far end of the pew stand up and walk to a small room near the altar. Then he came out and approached the altar where he kneeled. He said (what I would learn later) was a prayer of forgiveness and his penance.

Slowly one boy at a time got up and entered that room and repeated the process until it was finally my turn. So, I did the same and walked over to the room and entered. It was obvious I was supposed to kneel but after that I had no clue why I was there. Then I heard someone clear his voice from behind this fine cloth screen and I silently waited. It happened again. This time I responded: "Yes, can I help you?" Suddenly I heard an angry voice direct me to begin my confession. Not knowing what he meant I asked him to explain it. I heard a lot a yelling and a few expletive comments come from behind the thinly veiled screen. I heard a door slam and felt myself being jerked out of the small cubicle.

A big incident began to unfold where I would learn the meaning of confession and that I wasn't supposed to be in the confessional booth since I hadn't completed my first communion yet. (The nuns assumed because I was in the second grade that I had already finished my first communion.) Six months later I experienced my first communion. I've never forgotten how I felt the first time I went to confession. I just knew the priest knew it was me he was talking to as I was older than the rest of the kids. I assumed my list of sins to report was longer than the others and that would be the giveaway to the priest, however this wasn't the only myth I had from my first exposure to catholic school.

Don't ask me why but I had the notion that nuns wore black robes because they wanted to cover up the fact that they had pink legs. One day a gust of wind totally dispelled that concept. I saw that one nun's legs were white and in that instance, my world view changed. I realized that nuns are just normal people - no more, no less!

On the Move Again to New Orleans

It was time to move on again and this time involved a long train ride from California to New Orleans during the summertime. Yes, it was a very hot trip. Jo decided she needed to be near her family and work wasn't going well for either her or Herb at that time. Jo purchased a bucket of chicken to feed us on our long journey but it was gone a day early, forcing me to buy a sandwich off the food cart on the train. The sandwich had spoiled mayonnaise and I developed a bad case of food poisoning. (To this day I never buy pre-made sandwiches from vending machines.) The next three days I spent living in the bathroom as part of my first New Orleans experience. It's a shame I was ill because otherwise I would have loved the experience of riding a train from California to New Orleans.

During the next two years, we lived in Metairie, a suburb of New Orleans. I was now old enough to attend Jr. High School where I worked as a crossing guard. Even though I achieved the rank of Captain, I still had 3 occasions to be run down by drivers not paying attention. Fortunately, I was never injured in any of these drive-by run overs.

My next moment of fame happened when I was decorated for my service by the Sheriff of New Orleans and mayor. I was quite excited to receive the award and take pictures with them. (I felt it was worth almost getting run over to receive the award!)

Some tragic events that marked this time in my life, included the loss of my Grandfather, Dominic Pizzuto, and the assassination of John F. Kennedy in 1963.

Grandpa's Missing Palm Fronds

My Grandpa in New Orleans raised a small variety of palm trees in his back yard. Every Easter he cut the fronds and took them to the church to have them blessed. On the last Easter celebration that I shared with my Grandfather Dominic, he asked me to stay behind after mass, wait for the priest to bless his fronds, then bring them home. The whole family was at his house to celebrate the holiday and was waiting for my return.

The priest came and left with no sign of my Grandfathers palm fronds. I concluded that I would never get the blessing when I ran into a young couple with a baby outside of the church. They could see I had a problem and inquired. I explained the saga of the missing palms. They had two palm fronds that they had picked up after the blessing ceremony and offered one to me. I gladly accepted rather than go home empty handed. Later I found the missing fronds and gave the extra to someone else who was searching for one. That person was so thankful he gave me a silver dollar.

When I finally got home it took me an hour to explain about my exploits to the family. Despite the temporary misfortune, the whole experience ended up being very rewarding. That day I learned the value of how simple acts of kindness can spread out like the ripple of a stone on a quiet pond...when people help each other.

Losing Grandpa

My Grandpa was visiting us one day when he started having chest pains so we rushed him to the hospital. Jo had to leave me waiting alone in the hospital lobby to learn the outcome because in those days, children weren't allowed in treatment areas. The minute she stepped out of the elevator I knew that Grandpa was gone. She didn't need to say a word; her face gave it all away.

All I could think about was not being with him at the time he left this planet. I needed to tell him that I loved him, but now I would never get that chance. He had been the most stable male figure in my life and I worshipped the ground he walked on. One time I was left with Grandpa because my baby-sitter wanted to play with friends down the street. I wanted to go with her but he insisted I needed a nap. While he was in the garage working on some project, I put my clown doll in the bed and pulled the sheets up over its head. (The clown was about four feet tall and a perfect substitute for me.) Little did I know that grandpa would come inside after I left and be concerned because I had the sheets pulled over my head on a very warm day. He pulled them down to expose my head to fresh air only to discover that I was nowhere to be found. Later, after I finished playing with my friends I went back home and tried to act like I had just awoken, but my grandfather wasn't buying any of it.

Grandpa punished me by making me kneel on the linoleum kitchen floor with bare knees until my Mother got home from work. It was only about 15 minutes until she arrived, but it seemed like hours. That experience made a lasting impression on me and taught me to never get caught! I learned to develop skills to avoid discovery in the future and was generally quite successful.

Despite his moments of well-deserved discipline, losing my Grandfather left a hole in my life that will never be filled.

Second Chance at Catholic School

The time came for me to move to a different school. My parents enrolled me in another Catholic school, my second exposure to the religion.

During this time, my last name was Ela, same as Herb. At school, I learned that there was a famous king in biblical times name Eli. Whenever I saw a Nun, I was ready to hear the expression that sounded like: "Eli, Eli Sabado". I didn't know what it meant, but I heard it daily from the Nuns. I wasn't the perfect student, but for some reason I was well known by all the Nuns. (They always seem to know if I was up to something.)

My favorite Nun was Sister Mary Francis. She was young and I believed that I was in love with her. She could do no wrong in my eyes. One time she instructed me to do my homework that night and warned that if I failed, not to come to class the next day. I always had trouble with homework simply because it took away from playtime. (I certainly found playing with my friends to be more stimulating than homework.) I didn't do the assignment as instructed so the next day I decided to play hooky for my very first time. I rationalized that it was ok to stay away from school because she told me not to come if the work wasn't complete!

That morning I left the house as usual, but instead of school I went to the local park to spend the day. I had no idea that day would be one of the longest days of my life. It didn't take long to realize that I would be at the park all by myself because my friends were in school. Being alone was no fun at all. When I got hungry, I bought a hot dog from a vendor in the park. Eating lunch was the high point of my day otherwise I waited as the time slowly ticked away.

While I was hiding at the park, unbeknown to me one of the Nuns went to the bank where my mother worked to make a deposit for the church. She asked about my well-being since she hadn't seen me at school that day. To say Jo was surprised is putting it mildly. I was in for a big surprise.

On my way home, I stopped by the bank because we only lived less than a block from there. I walked in with a smile and acted like it had been a typical school day. Jo let me have it for skipping school and interrogated me for motive. I explained the reason why but she wasn't buying my excuse. She informed me that I had to meet with Mother Superior before I would be allowed back into class. The thought of having to see Mother Superior usually put the fear of God into any sane child. (Most kids believed that she was all powerful, omnipresent and rumor had it that once you went in her office you didn't come out!)

I believe you could have run a small city off the energy I released that morning as I sat outside her office waiting to be called for the inquisition. When she first entered the room, she asked if I wanted something to drink. Then she proceeded to tell me a joke. During my outburst of laughter, she slipped in the question: "do you ever intend to skip school again?" to which I responded: "definitely not". The entire experience left a bitter taste in my mouth and my behind wasn't too happy either after Herb got through with me.

Whenever, I was in trouble I had to wait for Herb to come home from work to face his anger and wrath. He had me strip naked and lay over the bed for a beating with a leather belt from my feet to my low back. I was black and blue and bloody when he was done. Strange it wasn't the pain that bothered me as much as the embarrassment and humiliation I felt from being forced to strip naked and expose myself. Maybe that was his intention. I still hadn't learned my lesson about getting caught quite yet but I never did skip school again!

Home Alone and Sick of the F.B.I

During the early 1960's I had a very bizarre incident during an outbreak of the Asian flu which was a national epidemic when I caught it.

I was sicker than a dog and spent an entire week in bed. I was home alone during the day of course, while everyone else was at work. I lay in bed with a severe headache and nausea, feeling like death would be a blessing. I was asleep for a little while when suddenly I was rudely frightened awake and found myself staring at the barrel of a 38-caliber handgun.

It appears the F.B.I. had a tip on a bookie operation and thought our house was the correct address. It wasn't but I had the living daylight scared out of me. The F.B.I. was very apologetic and paid for the repairs to our front door they busted down to gain entry. Perhaps, to this day it explains why I still get nervous when I see a cop in my rear-view mirror.

Odd Jobs of my Youth

I worked many odd jobs at an early age. I had newspaper routes, sold greeting cards door to door, cut lawns and sold used comic books to my cousin, among other jobs.

The comic books were a great deal for me. I'd buy them from the local barbershop owner, read them and then sell them to my cousin Warren. I paid a penny each and sold them for a nickel, earning a nice profit.

When I was 12 years old, I was hired to work at an animal hospital in New Orleans. I tried to convince the Vet that I was 14 and capable of working for him. He was a Mormon and told me up front that he would try to convert me to his religion. At first, he had no impact on me but eventually I become quite interested in his religion. The job itself was truly one of the best positions I have ever held. I assisted the Vet in surgery and cared for all the animals in the kennels. I remember fleas biting me so badly that I had to use dog flea shampoo to get rid of them. The only drawback to this job was when I had to assist with putting an animal to sleep. It always made me cry. I spent a little over a year at the animal hospital but it was the precursor of my career to become a Registered Nurse.

Shortly, after Hurricane Betsy hit New Orleans, I went to work at a local drive-in movie business and worked as ticket taker. I also put up the marquee each week.

I always desired to be responsible and work hard at all endeavors. That ethic always proved to be my saving grace. Work helped develop worth and I would achieve some level of self-esteem from working hard and giving my employers a day's work for a day's pay. Considering all the different jobs I would have, this manner of dealing with employers would eventually pay off for me in a big way.

During these years, I attended high school at a different school each year. At one point, I had four class rings. They made great presents to give to girls!

First Love

In 1967, 1 fell in love for the first time in my life, or at least I thought it was love. (It would be decades later before I experienced real love.) Her name was Debra. We were related as some sort of cousin, but because I was an orphan I didn't need to concern myself with that issue.

It was a true love story complete with real life drama that played out when I was forced to leave New Orleans with my parents to return to California. I fought as hard as any time in my life to stay, without success. My world was shattered; I was leaving the love of my life behind. Our relationship continued by mail for the next few years, but I learned that long distance relationships are nearly impossible to maintain.

Three years passed before I'd see Debra again and it was only a brief encounter. While in the Air Force I stopped in New Orleans with only a few hours to see her. I knew in an instant that our relationship had changed over time and distance. No matter how badly I wanted to go back I couldn't. I broke her heart the day I walked out. To this day, it is one of the few regrets I have. I know how much I hurt her and she didn't deserve to be treated that way. My only excuse is that I was a young male in heat using the wrong head to think with!

Thoughts of Self-Destruction

During this time in my life I tried to commit suicide for the first time. I've had thoughts of suicide since I was 8, but didn't make my first attempt until I was 12. I cut my arms but did a very poor job of it. I covered up the truth with a story of falling down a hill into a barrel cactus. (It's amazing what people believe if you are good at bullshitting!)

I learned that some people can be very gullible. I'm not sure why, (perhaps it was just one of my survival tools) but I certainly took advantage of that characteristic throughout my life. Perhaps it goes hand in hand with the concept that many people are followers. Only a few who are leaders take chances in this life. I always believed it was far better to lead then to follow because there is less dust to deal with in the back of the line!

Surviving several suicide attempts is one of the main reasons I write this book. Hopefully, it can help someone realize they aren't alone. Others in seemingly hopeless situations have proven they can survive if willing to except the changes required to abandon self-destructive thoughts. I now live believing that tomorrow always brings new possibilities and with it hope. It took some time before I found salvation. (No one ever accused me of being the sharpest tool in the shed!) What counts is that it eventually happened.

Be Responsible even if it Hurts

I was trained in my youth to behave. I was stressed every day of my life and learned that I must be responsible "at all times". I applied this rule to school, work and life in general. Failure to comply was never accepted and ended with a beating if I didn't. I believe subconsciously I lived with an inner driving force that motivated me to always comply because I owed a debt to the people who gave me a home. It was a constant reminder of my status as an orphan.

One incident occurred when I was about 8 that proved the seriousness of that structure in my life. One beautiful summer day the family was invited to a pool party. I loved to swim and loved spending the entire day in the pool. That afternoon I got out of the pool for something to drink. I walked toward the house and passed my mother who was in deep conversation with a guest. She called me to come over and I listened as she told this stranger how well I behaved and that bad behavior was not tolerated. To prove her point, she threw the lit cigarette she had been smoking on the ground and instructed me to step on it to put it out, knowing that I just gotten out of the swimming pool and was barefoot. Without hesitation, I ground that cigarette into oblivion with my foot. The cigarette stuck to the bottom of my wet foot so it kept burning.

I'm sure I looked quite comical hopping around like a Mexican jumping bean. She didn't show any concern at that time and I heard her state that she made her point and was quite pleased with herself. The stranger was equally impressed. Incidents like that taught me to always be vigilant, especially when in the public arena.

Learning to Always be on Guard

One time I was threatened by a neighbors' sons. The story goes that Jo and Herb had a friend named Roger. He was married to a strong woman who had a problem with alcohol and a tendency to beat him up every time she got drunk. Roger's wife also had issues with his alleged infidelities and had the notion that Jo and Herb were conspiring with Roger to cover up his indiscretions.

One nice spring morning I found myself in the middle of a dangerous situation that I had no concept how to handle. Roger's wife sent her two oldest sons (who were both much older than I) with instructions to beat me up because she thought my parents were assisting Roger. I was home alone (as usual) with two guys banging on the door and screaming that they intended to" kick my ass". To say I was scared would be an injustice.

I called my Mother and frantically told her what was going on. She knew it was the truth because she could hear the banging on the door over the telephone. She instructed me to keep the door locked and wait for someone to come and not to leave the house for any reason. (I had no problem following these orders.) Eventually, they grew tired of banging on our door and left, at which point I let out a big sigh of relief.

Serious incidents like this weren't that unusual for me to experience. Each time I faced a new dilemma, I managed to glean some tidbit of information that I learned to use at some future date to protect myself. Before I was an adult I had a library of defense tactics to use in any given situation. Survival became the most important aspect of my life and I believed should be a priority before all else. Years later I would learn how wrong I was on so many points, but at the time this approach seemed to work and suit me quite well.

One of the secrets I learned is that we must always be fluid in our approach to life and prepared to modify or change how we face every new challenge. What works today may not be effective in the future. Being flexible is essential to success.

Why was I Unwanted?

Life seemed to be a lonely proposition for me and (for the most part) I was void of self-esteem. Day in and day out I found myself alone and questioning why. The only answer I ever concluded was the simplest: I had no value and therefore, no one cared about me even though, somewhere in the back of my mind, I thought the purpose of having parents was to make one feel wanted, cared for and loved.

Because of the things I was exposed to up to this point, I didn't have the ability to trust anyone, including my parents. To make matters worse, Herb was nearing the end of his relationship with Jo and me. By the time I turned 12, Herb would be gone, succumbing to alcohol and gambling. I spent hours thinking of ways to end my life, because I just couldn't stand the feelings of loneliness and that the people around me never truly cared. Although there were brief moments in my everyday routines when I would be exposed to caring and love, they were short lived. I believed that people had their own agendas which motivated their actions towards me and that in the final analysis, it was best to watch my back. I played the game I referred to as "covering your ass".

By this stage in my growth and development I was fully aware that I had to provide for myself because I couldn't depend on someone else to do it. Additionally, I was cognizant of the fact that words people used and many things they said didn't seem to carry any weight.

Men entering my life as fathers promised to love and care for me, but their promises were empty and didn't last. After they were gone, as a rule, I never heard from them again...with the one exception being Herb. He broke that cycle when he contacted me ten or twelve years after he divorced Jo but even then, his motive was self-serving. As I previously mentioned, he asked me to take responsibility for him by signing him out of Patton State Hospital, where he had spent 5 years for killing my Uncle Donald. This situation proved to be one of the most challenging events of my life.

I plodded along in this world devoid of any sense of self-worth with the continuing question in my mind: Why didn't my real Mom and Dad want me? It's a question I'm sure other orphans ask themselves all the time. The problem is there is never an answer...just the question. Perhaps this was the motive behind my desire at an early age to die, perhaps so I would never have to feel that pain again.

I found myself fantasizing about my real parents. Maybe I was kidnapped from them. Maybe they were some famous family in America that couldn't afford the embarrassment of having a child out of wedlock so they were forced to give me away. I dreamed about them searching and coming for me with apologies and open arms, filled with love and attention.

My thoughts however, were nothing more than an exercise in futility, because in reality, I wasn't a secret Kennedy or Vanderbilt and no one was ever going to come and rescue me. Then I found myself feeling guilty because I had Jo and Herb. Why was I thinking about these mystery people who didn't even want to meet me?

In retrospect, I know I suffered from Depression (just like 20 million other Americans), but I didn't know it was that at the time. I lived most my life hiding my depression from the world which during my youth was rather easy, considering the world I lived in. Most people in my circle of life were too pre-occupied with themselves. Looking back, I realize I didn't have a prayer they would even notice.

Time to Say Goodbye to Herb

Herb worked in the food service industry most of his time with us and developed great skill as a Mixologist. The title sounds impressive but in reality, he was just a good bartender. He once had the privilege of serving President John F. Kennedy on one of his trips to Palm Springs to play golf with Frank Sinatra and the rest of the" Rat Pack". I remember that day and how proud I was of him. After that event, I wrote President Kennedy a letter.

Eventually, Herb made the biggest mistake any bartender could make. He started testing and consuming his own products. It took years but eventually he became an alcoholic. To compound the problem, he also became a compulsive gambler. At the time of his decline, I was earning a decent money for a kid during those days. Sure enough, Herb found the dresser drawer where I hid my hard-earned money and started stealing from me.

The final nail in this relationship was when Jo found out that he mortgaged her mothers' antique furniture for drinking and gambling funds. I wish I had a picture of Jo's face the day she came home from work and I told her that some men with a moving truck came earlier with the intention of repossessing her furniture. Shortly after that day, Herb was history. (Never fear, I had a replacement Dad before the ink was dry on the divorce papers.)

To complicate matters, before Jo started the divorce process, she discovered that Dennis, her former husband, had never completed their divorce. In fact, she was still legally married to him. Dennis had never paid child support payments and he used that as leverage against Jo and agreed to the divorce only if she released him from his obligation for the past due payments. Dennis won out and she got her freedom to marry the next poor slob. So, as we end Herb's ugly involvement with Jo and me, I found the concept that you can never trust people reinforced.

Father Number Three

Herb was barely out the door and here came my new father, number three, Ron. He was a devoted Catholic from New Orleans who first met Jo while he was married to his first wife. Herb hadn't faded from memory yet and here was a new stranger that I was forced to get to know and behave as though I liked him. Ironically, I hated him at first, mainly because I didn't want to start yet another father-son relationship all over again.

Ron was an instructor at the local community college teaching auto mechanics. His first wife (a good Catholic girl from New Orleans) had five children with Ron ranging in ages 1 to 8 years old. The kids were nice and I certainly didn't hold anything against them but I didn't care for a man who was willing to walk out on five kids for another woman, even if that other woman was my mother.

Jo's family on the other hand presented me with a unique problem. They didn't care for Ron either and constantly told me their negative assessments of him (as if I could do something about this mess). One night just before Ron moved in with us I asked my Mother why she was committing to this man so soon after Herbs' departure? I never forgot her response. She said that she didn't know how to live in this world on her own and she needed a man in her life. Then she admitted that she didn't even love this guy. To say I was confused is an enormous understatement.

We moved around the area of New Orleans for a couple of years before Ron crushed my world. He announced we were moving back to California so he could take a position selling cemetery plots. I did increase my knowledge of jokes, especially those that dealt with death. (It's ironic that the subject of death was always in the back of my mind.) The fact remains that a person I barely knew (or cared about) uprooted me from MY life, without even talking it over with me. Afterwards, I struggled in my relationship with Ron. It would be close to 5 years before I found common ground with him, only to have yet another father figure leave a few years later.

Leaving New Orleans was devastating. I never fully recovered from that relocation. It's where I had my first love and a great job working for the local Drive-In Theater. The company was building the first Movie Multiplex in the area and I was promised a position in management training. It seemed that no matter what was important to me it always took a back seat to everyone else.

Once again, I found myself in a new environment, struggling to make new friends and a new life. I am thankful that Ron took the time to help me with my weight problem. Just before the start of my junior year in high school, Ron said if I didn't figure out how to lose the weight now, in my youth, it would only get harder with age. Thanks to that simple comment, I immediately made up my mind to act. We lived in Thousand Oaks, California where I had my first exposure to cross-country and I decided this was the best way to shed all those extra pounds. It worked better than expected and by the conclusion of the season, I had trimmed down from 220 pounds at 5 feet

8 inches tall to 135 pounds in about three months. I lost too much too fast however, which made me sick. Near the end of the cross-country season and within about a month, I had regained about 20 pounds and felt much better.

I was the heaviest boy on my team by more than 50 pounds which even included all the seniors. My self-goal was to never be last in any race that I ran which I fulfilled, including practice runs. By the end of the season (in the last race of the year) I surpassed my own goal and scored a point in the team competition by finishing number 8 in the race. I finally found some merit in having Ron as a father figure as he was the motivator for me to lose the weight but his time with my family was also drawing to close (even though he didn't know it at the time).

Lessons of Constant Change

With our return to California around 1967, I attended several new schools and was forced to adjust and make new friends on a regular basis. Each time I was involved with a different group of kids. At one school, I might be in tight with the academic crowd...the "nerdy" or goody two shoes types. In another school, it would be the rough group...the kids on campus known for getting into trouble. My trick for getting into a new group was to always keep my mouth shut, until I had a feel for what the group found to be important and then I emulated the appropriate behavior. I used this same technique as an adult with any new position I took. Living life in this manner wasn't without pitfalls. I found out much later in life that people often thought I was standoffish and egotistical.

School Daze

I attended a different school in each year of high school. I tried to take a typing class one year but only lasted a whole week before I withdrew. I was the only male in class and went nuts listening to all the girls talk about their boyfriends. When I withdrew, the only other class open to me was the school choir. I got an "A" in this class, not because I had a great voice, but rather the best work ethic.

Our choir was very involved in the community so I always had plenty of special projects to work on. My favorite experience with the choir was our trip to Camarillo State Hospital where we spent the day caring for young children from abused backgrounds. I remember when the instructor informed us that they didn't have enough kids to go around. That meant there wouldn't be anyone for me to spend the day with when we all went to the zoo that afternoon. Just when I had given up hope, I was informed that there was one kid left but concern because of his behavior and multiple psychiatric problems. I was given the choice to accept this young man or simply tag along for the day. I jumped at the chance to accompany their number one problem child for the day. It was a challenge I just couldn't pass up.

The young man turned out to be very pleasant except for his bizarre behavior. When we arrived at the zoo the first thing he did was run up to the fountain in front and proceed to urinate in the pond. Next, I caught him eating ice cream that someone had dropped on the ground. During our lunch break, all was going well until he suddenly jumped up at the table screaming at the top of his lungs, saying that the world was coming to an end with ten million tanks. This scared the other kids but I found it somewhat interesting! He spent the entire day rambling about all sorts of fanciful ideas. My favorite was that he was going to start a rock and roll band with everyone that lived-in Burbank and all would play an electric guitar.

It may come as a surprise but I found my heart breaking when I said goodbye to him that day. I never forgot how he stood alone outside the dorm watching as we drove away, just waving goodbye and holding the stuffed animal I bought for him at the zoo. He touched my soul the way few people have in this life and I often wonder what became of him.

My school year would be interrupted again when my "parents" informed me at Christmas that we were going to move yet again, this time back to the desert. I threw a fit and stated that under no terms was I going to leave school in the middle of the year. Fortunately, my very best friend Nancy was there to step up for me. She spoke to her parents about letting me stay with them until I finished the year and they agreed. So, my family left me and headed for the desert while I stayed behind to finish the year. When summer came, I joined them in Palm Springs.

I lost touch with Nancy for several years and when I finally tracked her down, found out she had married and then lost her husband to cancer before he was 30 years old. I felt great sympathy for her and wished I could have been there for her like she had been for me, but this was not to be. We lost track of each other again.

I must admit living in the desert was an easy transition this time because we lived there before and I still had a few friends. This time I was in with the tough guy group. We weren't that bad but because I came from Desert Hot Springs, the kids who lived in Palm Springs treated us differently. I didn't mind because I had no desire to hang out with a bunch of spoiled rotten rich kids.

I eventually graduated from Palm Springs High School but my time there (as most everywhere) was not without its trials and tribulations. Prior to the end of the school year, we were instructed to bring in all outstanding textbooks or we wouldn't be allowed to graduate. I took care of this responsibility a.s.a.p. because I had no desire to be around those people any longer than necessary! On graduation night, I proudly sat in the bleachers waiting for my name to be called. I ascended the stairs to receive my diploma, the principal handed me the folder, we shook hands and I left the stage. After returning to my seat, I opened the folder to get my first glance at the one document I had been in search of all these years. When I did, I found a note stating my diploma was being held hostage until I returned an outstanding book for my "Boy Chef" class. Immediately following the ceremony, I was feeling rage and frustration because I knew I had turned in every book I had and I was right. I approached the principal who informed me he couldn't access the documents as they were secured in a safe and he didn't have the combination. I couldn't believe they were doing this to me. I believe I even threatened the man! I had no intention of going home empty-handed to the party that awaited my arrival but that is exactly what happened. The next day I received my diploma and an apology from the principal but the party was a complete wash for me!

After I graduated from high school I attended college but decided I couldn't get away from the academic world fast enough. The Viet Nam War was in full swing at the time and I became one of those who served.

The Lonely and Famous Offer Opportunity

I begin this chapter in my life and my story by saying that, whether adopted or not, everyone has good and bad experiences. I debated for some time whether to include this part of my story. I struggled with the idea of exposing this shameful part of my life but after speaking with my wife and a few friends I decided to include it.

Shortly after I turned 16 years old, my parents planned a weekend trip to the coast, and left me at home to paint my bedroom. They had no sooner left and I started calling my friends to plan a party. That night I made a fatal error by calling my folks frequently, inquiring where they were on their trip. That, of course, sent up red flags and they returned home early, before I had time to clean up all the evidence. Someone stole some of my mothers' make-up and one young lady spent time in their bed during her menstrual cycle, leaving an unwanted surprise on the sheets.

Ron was furious and chased me into the desert, with treats of death and informed me that I had to move out that night. So, at 16, I was on my own. At first, I thought it was no big deal...that I could survive without their help. Soon I discovered that finishing the last year of high school and supporting myself at my age wasn't the piece of cake I assumed it would be.

I had a job working at the local car agency and acquired another as a valet parking attendant. As a parking attendant, I met and served many famous people. It wasn't uncommon to make several hundred dollars in tips on any given night. One night Frank

Sinatra and his girlfriend (at the time) arrived for dinner in separate limousines. I parked their limos and waited for them to enjoy the meal. When I knew patrons were near completion, I would retrieve their limos and have them ready with engines running, headlights on and doors open, waiting for their expedient departures. To my shock, I found that I had parked Mr. Sinatra's limo on a broken bottle and the tire was completely flat. In a mad rush, I pulled out the spare tire and changed the flat.

When they came out, I immediately explained what had happened and the girlfriend reacted like I had just completed brain surgery or some other spectacular feat! Frank proceeded to give me a hundred-dollar tip, something he did often in those days. It was an exciting job for a young man like me. I also saw stars like Kirk Douglas, Bob Hope, Richard Burton, Danny Thomas, Elizabeth Taylor and others.

Despite the two jobs, I still wasn't making enough to cover all my basic needs. I had a series of unfortunate events that happened and I found myself in a dire strait financially. I didn't want to go crawling back to the family on my hands and knees, begging for forgiveness and help. In fact, I was determined not to go back home since it wasn't my choice to be thrown out, at such an early age to begin with.

Then a new opportunity presented itself. One night after my shift I found myself at the bar where I worked my valet job, having a drink with the head Maître' d. (Yes, I know I was only 16 years old but mature enough to convince people that I was 21. Thus, I enjoyed many Navy Grogs or Mai Tai drinks at their bar!) Roy was his name and he was a dancer, years earlier in the days of vaudeville and then an aid to a general during WWII. He propositioned me one night when I was most vulnerable and in need of cash fast. This was the start of my next job, that of male prostitute.

I take no pride or shame in this phase of my life, because I was only 16. The world can be a harsh place in which to survive when you are young, vulnerable and living on your own. It wasn't the typically bad experience you hear today about kids who are forced to prostitute themselves. I made a great deal of money, which immediately ended all my financial problems and I prospered. Most importantly, I was lucky that no one ever tried to hurt me, as they were generally people of power and wealth. Overall the experience was a positive one for me and because I would soon start college, I discovered my new-found wealth to be a major asset.

This job provided all the security I ever needed and taught me a lot about people. I learned that there are many people in this world who feel alone. The fact that so many people need simple human contact and would spend any amount necessary to have what they want (or think they need) always amazed me. I learned that no matter how much money or power a person has it doesn't mean they are happy with their lives even if they have people who genuinely care about them. From those experiences, I learned lessons that would help me understand people around me in my everyday life.

Throughout my life I would have contact with many people who were in some way, connected to the worlds' most famous and/or infamous people. Roy was one of them. Our friendship would lead to a close encounter with relics of Adolph Hitler. During WWII Roy was quartered in a villa in France that was a summer home for Eva and Hitler. As a result, he acquired some of their personal belongings. I ended up with a cigarette tray with a sculpture of a naked lady on top that had belonged to Hitler and a plate from the china set used by Eva. The plate became part of my mother's collection some years later. It was eventually sold to an individual who bought my parents restaurant business. I often wonder if that person realizes the value of what they own and to whom it belonged.

Joining the Air Force

In March of 1969, I left that part of my life behind and joined the Air Force. Our nation was in conflict and it was at a time when the war in Viet Nam wasn't going well.

I received a letter from the draft service informing me that I had failed to register and that my non-action could lead to a large fine and/or ten years in jail. I didn't hesitate to comply and drove to San Bernardino to the local recruiters' office. I was born on base at Camp Pendleton and it had always been my goal to join the Marine Corps but instead, I walked right past the Marine recruiter and headed for the Air Force. To this day, I have no knowledge of why I did that. My choice certainly wasn't to save myself, because as soon as I entered the Air Force I volunteered for Nam.

I took all the military exams for placement and I tested best in mechanics although I had never been particularly adept at working on machines. Whenever I tried to fix anything I always ended up with parts left over and generally that item never worked again but I was still willing to try!

If I passed the physical I would be sworn in and shipped off to boot camp. When I was 16 and working for the Cadillac agency, I had fractured my back at T - 10 and wore a brace for about a year to recover from the injury. They asked if I had any back problems and I told them what happened. Immediately, I was sent to see the Orthopedic Surgeon for evaluation. After the exam, I found myself on the floor on my hands and knees, in boxer shorts, in front of a full bird Colonel, begging him to let me in, while many recruits were trying to find ways to get out of service. The Colonel looked at me and said: "Son, I've been in this business for twenty years and no one has ever begged me to let them join the military. So frankly, I don't care if you are fit for service or not...I'm going to let you in."

Immediately he signed my papers with a 1-A status and I was on my way to Lackland Air Force Base in San Antonio, Texas. This would begin the best years of my life where I developed a sense of self- worth thanks to Tommie, my recruiter and mentor in the Air Forces Special Forces branch. This branch is called Para-rescue Service and was attached to the Aerospace Rescue and Recovery Service. The training and process takes over a year to complete and the odds of succeeding were stacked against me.

On day one, Tommie handed me the pamphlet which stated that only 8 out of every 10,000 recruits who volunteer to be a Pararescueman (known as P.J.s) survive to complete the training and awarded the Maroon Beret. He stood on the stage that day wearing a full leg cast, walking with crutches. Tommie was a genuine hero. He was blown out of a HH-43 helicopter while attempting fire suppression for a B-52 which had a bomb stuck in the Bombay doors as it attempted to land. He should not have survived (and in fact "died" several times on the table) or walk again. The surgeons didn't realize they were dealing with a Pararescueman! Tommie's unit was the most decorated in the Viet Nam War. He eventually regained his flight and jump status and returned to full duty. We used to say, "God created P.J.'s...then came the rest"!

I passed the land physical training and then the water evaluation. In the water evaluation, we had to swim a mile in less than 1 hour and pass an Oxygen tolerance test. If you made it that far you were scheduled for the next class. In between completion of boot camp and P.J. training, I was placed in charge of a discharge barracks for men who had declared themselves homosexual (not allowed in those days) and men who had washed out of officer training. One guy failing officer training had a degree in nuclear physics and another professed homosexual was a violinist from the San Francisco Philharmonic Orchestra. I became friends with the former and he was the person who taught me how to play Rummy, a card game that I love to this day. I have been playing an ongoing game of rummy with my wife for 17 years.

Jo came to visit when I graduated.

Proud Pararescueman

A bit of historical background: With the advent of air warfare it became increasingly clear that the military needed a system for recovering downed pilots in combat. Initially, physicians were used for this project, but the loss of a valuable physician in combat led to the concept of training enlisted men to perform emergency medical care.

In May of 1945, the 8th E.R.S. (Emergency Rescue Service) was formed in China and became the first A.A.F. (Army/Air Force) unit. By 1946, the E.R.S. became A.R.S. (or Air Rescue Service) under the authority of the Air Transport Command. Their responsibility was to provide rescue coverage for the entire continental United States with the primary mission being military rescue and recovery but also included civilian rescue, as well.

In 1949, the service was expanded to cover the worlds transport routes. In 1966, the A.R.S. would be re-designated as A.R.R.S. (or Aerospace Rescue and Recovery Service). The purpose was to reflect changing roles and the introduction of space travel and necessary recovery operations. I served with the Aerospace Rescue and Recovery Service.

During the Vietnam era, Para rescue service personnel received more decorations per capita than any other group or organization in the Air Force. They completed more than 4120 rescues (with 2780 of those missions in combat situations). Pararescuemen are known by the distinctive Maroon Beret, which represents the universal color for rendering medical aid as well as symbolizing sacrifice. The crest on the beret depicts the Angel of Mercy wearing a parachute and holding the globe of the earth. Part of our motto: "that others may live" is taken from the line "these things we do that others may live". The unit patch, Air Rescue Service Shield, worn on the uniform sleeve, has a field of blue to represent the sky with the golden light as a ray of hope for those in need. An Angel in Red Robe represents protection and rescue from harms' way. The red symbolizes valor displayed by Pararescueman around the globe for their humanitarian deeds. An example of the value of one P.J. is the fact that only two captured enlisted men were held at the Hanoi Hilton (which housed the officer core) and both were P.J.

It would be easy to write a book about the Para rescue Service, but that isn't the focus of this book. However, I would be remiss if I didn't tell you a few good war stories and some of the opportunities I was afforded during my service. In the very early days of my career as a P.J. someone was wise enough to tell me to take advantage of what the Air Force could and must offer and to get as much training as possible. I followed that advice with a total of 17 formal schools of training during my enlistment. This paid off for me when I returned to college after service. I was awarded 14 full credits for my experience which made completing college that much easier.

Para Rescue Missions Accomplished

On my very first mission I was assigned to the rescue squadron at Clark Air Base in the Republic of the Philippines. One sunny afternoon while resting in the alert room I got word we were being scrambled for a mission to rescue a private pilot. He had crashed in the jungle about 15 minutes due west of our location. So, off I went on a mission that I had desired since graduating P.J. school. This was my first opportunity to use the skills I learned over the last year and a half.

Based on our intelligence, we easily located the pilot who crashed near a village. Our pilot landed the HH-3 helicopter in a field and I immediately hit the ground running in search of my patient. It took less than 5 minutes to locate the pilot who crashed more than 24 hours earlier. He had crawled more than a mile to the village with 90% body burns. His burns were full thickness (or third-degree). All I could do when I saw him was what one Major taught me in medical school. If you reach a victim and you feel overwhelmed, drop to the ground and do 25 push-ups, then proceed to take care of the patient. (All through school I thought he was nuts for telling us to do that, but he was right.)

The pilot was so severely burned I didn't know where to begin. I did the 25 push-ups (which meant nothing to him even if he was aware) but it gave me time to collect my thoughts and develop a plan of action. My first important decision was how to establish an intravenous (IV) route to provide hydration and administer medications (such as pain medication or antibiotics). Due to the severity of his injuries it was obvious he needed what is referred to as a "cut down" to establish the access. This requires a minor surgical procedure that takes at least 15 to 20 minutes to accomplish. We were only 14 minutes away from advanced medical care at the base hospital so I elected to transport immediately. It proved to be the right choice and the aircraft commander was in full agreement with my plan. The pilot survived three more days but died due to massive infections.

My second mission involved one of the weirder requests during my service as a P.J. Once again, I was waiting for some poor soul to have an accident who would need my skills when I get word that I was needed in the squadron briefing room. On arrival, I was briefed that the Philippine government had requested our assistance with reconnaissance of a nearby volcanic mountain, Mount Pinatubo, which was due west of Clark Air Base. I found it interesting that I was asked to perform tasks for which I had never been prepared. It seems the local Government Geologist was concerned about the amount of activity they were seeing from the mountain. So, off we went into the wild blue yonder. As soon as we reached the volcano, the pilot lowered the aircraft down into the crater and I started taking pictures of its interior. It was a very strange, surrealistic experience for me, to say nothing of the fact that it smelled like rotten eggs from the sulfur blowholes releasing fumes. It would be years later before Pinatubo would finally blow. I wonder what became of the film I shot that afternoon.

My first Viet Nam mission request came during the second Tet offensive in the spring/summer 1972. I was assigned to Det. 14 TSN, Vietnam. My Squadron Commander called me into his office in the alert shack and proceeded to tell me that a pilot had been shot down just north of the base (that bordered the city of Saigon). There was concern that the North Vietnamese would retrieve the aircraft black box. I was briefed by an electronics expert on what needed to be done to remove the black box. Apparently, he wasn't willing to go himself and that is the reason I was picked. The mission went well and I recovered the device.

After I finished my time in Vietnam, some three or four months in country plus 18 months flying aerial command support in operation "Duck Butt". I received an Air Medal for flying 24 combat rescue missions, along with other service ribbons for Vietnam.

Non-Combat Rescue Missions

During the Christmas holiday of 1973, I volunteered to take the alert watch so the married staff could be with their families. On Christmas Eve, I was scrambled for a mission to rescue a lost scuba diver. Before I could clean up from that mission, we were scrambled again, this time to locate a mother and newborn baby who apparently wasn't thriving. The woman was married to an American so we were sent south to render aid. We landed on an airstrip left over from WWII that wasn't quite as long as the pilot preferred, however, he did a good job of getting us down safely.

Upon arrival, the pilot and I rented a local Jeep and drove in the direction of the waiting mother. Along the way we passed an ambulance that was transporting the mother and baby so we turned around and followed the ambulance back to the aircraft where I began my assessment. I determined the baby had an intestinal blockage and was unable to hold down any nutrition. I provided as much care as I was prepared for, considering I was trained in emergency medicine for use in traumatic situations and not pediatric emergencies. My greatest accomplishment that afternoon was successfully changing a diaper while landing in an HC-130 turbo-prop without getting anything on myself or sticking the baby with the diaper pin! I considered this an outstanding mission, perhaps because it was the Christmas season.

This last story I will tell involves the eventual crash of the aircraft I was on for a mission. Once again, I was on alert when communication came in that a Chinese freighter captain hadn't urinated in 5 days. The ship he was on was at least two weeks away from its destination port. So, off we went, some 150 miles off the coast, due west of the base. When we arrived, it was obvious that I would have to be lowered to the deck with the helicopter hoist. The flight mechanic lowered me and immediately I was surrounded by a group of Chinese sailors, none who spoke English.

I tried sign language in an attempt to find out where the captain was located. Shortly after, I saw a small group of men coming toward me from the center of the ship. It was the captain being aided by several crewmembers because he couldn't walk. I lowered the seat on the penetrator, secured the skipper, pulled down a seat for myself and gave the hand signal to the flight mechanic to bring us up. I can only imagine what the Chinese captain must have thought under these circumstances. Riding on a penetrator over 150 feet up can be quite frightening. The cable that holds you is only a quarter of an inch in diameter and tends to disappear when you look up towards the aircraft but he did quite well for his first ride.

Once on board, care was rendered and we headed back towards the base. Shortly after, I looked up at the window closest to me and noticed a stream of hydraulic fluid flowing over the window, heavy enough to totally obstruct my view. I immediately called the pilot to inform him of the situation and he directed the flight mechanic to evaluate the problem. As the mechanic started to diagnose the problem, the engine seized and we began to fall from the sky like a rock. The pilot maintained his composure and used the technique of autorotation to safely land the aircraft at sea. When we hit the water, I believe I lost a filling or two and another inch in height.

According to Air Force regulations following a crash, I became the de facto commander of the mission, because I was a survival expert. I launched the 7-man life raft and gave the order to abandon the aircraft, while the mechanic and I stayed aboard utilizing the bilge pumps. The next time I looked for the crew they were gone--- floating away from the aircraft. The pilot had radioed our situation and position to our base and they dispatched an HC-130 to our location. Upon arrival, they dropped the MA1 kit. This is several bundles of equipment with life rafts, food and survival supplies but the bundles were down wind of our location. At this point the crew was in one raft about a mile away from my location and the survival equipment is floating away from us in the wrong direction. This is when I thought of my hero, John Wayne, and asked myself what he would do! The answer was simple: get in the water and swim to the survival gear, collect it and then swim to the raft holding the crew and patient. I pulled off my flight suit and quickly remembered that all that I was wearing underneath was a jock strap. I grabbed my fins and mask and went into the water. After only a few strokes, I remembered that I was in shark-infested water, specifically, the home of the Great White shark. I calmed my fear quickly by focusing on the "Duke" and how he would have behaved.

Eventually, the Navy sent a helicopter from Subic Bay. When they picked us up I was only wearing my fins, mask and jock strap. It was news for the Navy to rescue an Air Force crew so the local reporter for the Navy Times was waiting for us when we landed at the base. I climbed out of the aircraft and waited for another crewmember to hand the Chinese captain down to my waiting arms. He was so scared when he exited the helicopter that he wrapped his legs around my neck and hung onto my head like it was a floatation device. I might have thought it was amusing if not for a Navy Times reporter clicking pictures as fast as his finger could accomplish. I'm sure I must have made the front page and provided the local swab jockeys with a good laugh or two.

The pilots got a ride and the ambulance left with the patient. That left me standing on the tarmac almost naked (just that jock strap), along with the flight mechanic. We decided we were hungry, so off we went to the operations building where the cafeteria was located. Just as I walked through the front door, I ran into several wives of local Navy pilots waiting for their husbands, no doubt. I ignored them and headed for the cafeteria where I promptly asked for a hamburger and fries. You should have seen the look on the face of the cashier, as I stood there wearing only my jock strap, thinking that she certainly must suspect I didn't have any money to pay. Fortunately, she realized what had just occurred and extended me credit. I got my burger, sat down and ate my meal with the mechanic. Finally, after a long day, I headed back to my base with a ride from a good Samaritan.

For my actions, my commander recommended me for a Distinguished Flying Cross, but it was downgraded because of politics. I received an Air Medal with Oak

Leaf Cluster. The aircraft investigation team wanted to find someone to blame and I was thoroughly interrogated. For two weeks, I tried to account for every action, meal, drink and how much I slept, in addition to all types of personnel interactions. Remembering every little detail was not easy. The way I looked at it was I had survived and that was a perfect closure to my experience. Unfortunately, the commander of the mission was eventually blamed for the loss of the aircraft.

The Air Force afforded me the opportunity to travel to the Orient and Europe, as well as the U.S. and along the way, I met many fine people. Other experiences of note include my part in the Apollo Recovery program where I did stand-by for three different Apollo landings. In another mission, I met Charles Lindberg after a good friend rescued him lost in the southern Philippines. I also had the great privilege of greeting returning P.O.W.s when they landed at Clark Air Base. I'll never forget that walk through the base's hospital ward and seeing the walls covered with hand drawings made by the children of base personnel. It was very inspiring. But perhaps my proudest moment of all was when I flew support coverage for President Richard Nixon on his historic trip to mainland China.

During my Air Force days, the training I participated in included interaction with the Army, Navy, Coast Guard, German Red Cross (Bergwacht) and Marines (when I attended Jump school). Just before my departure I received a Civilian award called the "Winged 'S'", from Sikorsky Aircraft Company for participation in a record setting mission. The HH-3 helicopter I flew in traveled more than 500 miles over open water at night; rescued two dozen sailors and an orangutan. We set a record for night over water refueling of a helicopter. I suppose the record still stands to this day.

The Air Force was the best thing I did with my life. I think it's safe to say that I too was rescued (from abortion), to complete this part of my destiny, which was rescuing others.) I planned to make it my career, but that was not the path I followed. My career ended on the demand of my family. They insisted they needed my help with the family restaurant. After pulling my responsibility string they talked me into leaving the love of my life: Para rescue! I reluctantly departed the service, unaware at the time that in 12 years (from that day) I would find myself in the U.S. Navy.

Now I was on my way home to spend my life as a civilian, working in the family business. Little did I know about an event that would occur within one year of my return and how it would impact my life in a major way.

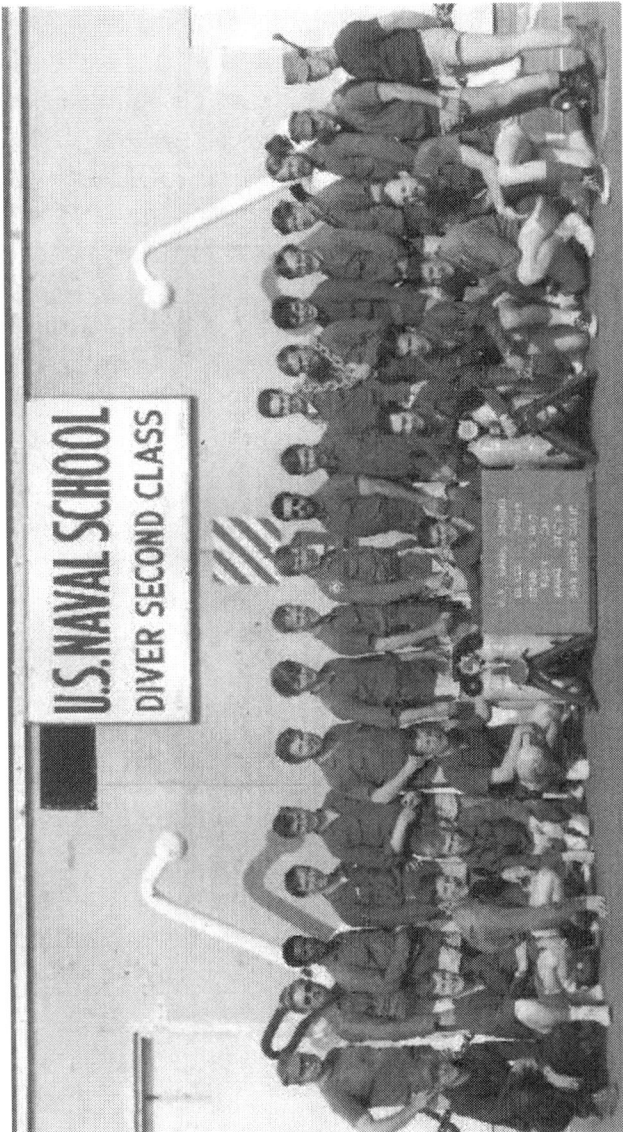

Spouse Number 3: Breaking up is Hard

Ron decided he should teach me how to be a Fry Cook. Within 2 months, I was putting him to shame and this created a little friction between us. Shortly after I became proficient at cooking, Ron and Jo started taking a lot of mini-vacations, leaving me behind to run the business. By the end of that year the next calamity was about to smack me right between the eyes. It was time for a family reshuffle.

Ron came to me one fine day with a story about how he was involved with another woman. He explained that he planned a separate vacation this year from Jo and that she was planning her own. He was telling Jo that he was going fishing in Washington State but instead was planning a trip to England to meet his mistress. To make matters worse, the woman he was having the affair with was Jo's best friend (and wife of Ron's best friend). Jo and Ron usually spent at least two or three nights a week with these friends.

I decided it wasn't my business to get in the middle, and as adults, this was something they had to work out themselves. (The only reason Ron told me was because he was planning to sell the restaurant and I needed to know how to reach him if a buyer showed up with a valid offer.) I grew to regret my silence in this matter because trouble somehow always found its way back to me as the responsible party (as if it was my fault that the affair had occurred).

I debated for some time whether to tell Jo what was going on. She wasn't in a healthy frame of mind in those days and was taking a hand full of Psych drugs on a regular basis. I was concerned that if she found out it would be too hurtful for her to deal with. I decided it was best to let her take her vacation to New Orleans where she planned to visit family. I thought perhaps a couple of months away might give her the mental strength to deal with yet another failed marriage. My plan didn't work out quite as I had intended. According to her, I was more evil than Ron and his mistress. It seems that both Jo and the spurned husband shared the opinion that I should have told them so they could have used the time that Ron and his mistress were away to take care of money matters and change the locks on the house before they returned.

It was a very ugly split and everyone involved did their best to suck me into this mess. The real irony here is that after the divorce, Ron and his mistress moved into their new home and her husband Eli, moved in with Jo and lived together the next 8 or 9 years until his death from an Abdominal Aneurysm. To this day, they have never forgiven me for not telling them what was going on. Perhaps they are correct, but I had my own life to worry about and because of their actions I was out of the service and a job (because they sold the restaurant). I considered going back into the Air Force, but I had long since learned that if you go back, nothing is ever the same. So now I needed to decide what to do for the rest of my life. I struggled with believing I was deserving, as I now carried the haunting guilt that I always seem to make the wrong choices at the wrong time.

Jim as a Chef

Moving on to School Days Again

I took inventory of my military service and it became quite clear that some of my skills for employment were not very useful. I researched Smoke Jumping for the Fire Service, commercial diving and giving tours to outdoorsman. None of these options using my military skills seemed very practical in terms of longevity. (Both smoke jumpers and commercial divers have short careers and take a toll on the body.)

The only option that made sense to me was to take advantage of my medical background. I enrolled in a Nursing School program where I found an opportunity to use my military service knowledge. The program I attended had a paramedic-training program for local E.M.T.'s, but no instructor to provide training. One instructor in the nursing program was aware of my background and saw that I was terribly bored simply because I already had training and skills as a paramedic. She suggested that I apply for the position as an instructor and I was accepted.

I applied for a teaching credential that took less than a month to accomplish. Strangely I was hired to teach as a college instructor while attending nursing school in the same department. (Some of my fellow instructors were upset because I had 2 mailboxes (one as a student and one as an instructor) and they only had one. One instructor raised a concern that as an instructor I had a full set of keys to the department, but I needed it because I frequently taught class on the weekends. Her concern was that I had access to the exams for the nursing program and that I might steal them to aid myself in passing the program. I met with the Dean of the Nursing and explained that I was there for an education and cheating wasn't going to teach me anything. Then I reminded her that cheating now wouldn't help me pass state board exams for my Nursing license if I didn't know the material. She fully agreed and that was the end of that incident.

Nursing school wasn't much different than the military except I was 25 years old and most of my classmates were in their teens. I was selected to be the class president because of my time in service and rank. I was in charge but don't be too impressed with the title, because it was mostly just that: a title. One other guy in my class had been in the service also but he had no desire to lead the class. We had six men and 30 women in my class (a couple females were over the age of 30).

I encountered problems in the nursing program early in the training. Instructors were teaching things I already learned in the military so I was easily bored. An example during my first semester was the first time I had to administer oral medications for patients at the local hospital. My instructor was in her first year of teaching and had worked her way up the ladder as an aid and upgraded to L.V.N. status. (Eventually she became an R.N.) That morning we arrived at the Medical Center at 6 a.m. for our assignments. I was placed on the Ortho Unit to pass out the 10 a.m. medication for patients on the unit. I still had more of a military mindset than a civilian at this point. I go to the unit and proceed to pour all medications, check, double and triple check to make sure there were no mistakes. By 9:30 a.m. that morning I called my instructor to inform her that my pour was complete. I needed her to inspect my work and watch me administer the medications. I watched the clock and waited for her arrival. By 10:15 a.m. she hadn't arrived and didn't respond to her pager. All I could think about was the Doctor had ordered these meds to be given at 10 a.m., I was late, and out of compliance with his orders. I took the initiative and asked the Charge Nurse on my unit to check my medications for accuracy. She was a graduate of the same nursing program and familiar with the schools' standards and policies. She promptly checked my medications and found no errors. I told her of my intent to dispense so I wouldn't be any later than I was.

My instructor showed up with a smile sometime around 11 am and said: "let's go check your meds so you can get your med pass completed". I immediately informed her that the Doctor had ordered these drugs to be given at 10 a. m. and I wasn't going to be late and possibly harm some patient. I explained how the charge nurse checked and cleared me for passing out the drugs. She grabbed my arm and pulled me into a closed room off the unit. She asked if I had dispensed the meds, and if so, why didn't I wait for her to come. I told her that I had no intention of delaying medications that patients needed simply because she couldn't manage her time better. She looked at me with a look of frustration and said: "Jim let's keep this between us and just promise me that you will never do that again". I agreed and went about my business the rest of the day. That was the last time it was mentioned.

After I finished the nursing program we became very close and developed a special relationship but I did give her one more fit before the semester was over. The entire semester I was supposed to make medication cards for each new drug we dispensed so that we could learn about the drug and any potential problems or interactions with other medications. I personally thought it was stupid to spend time looking up a drug in the P.D.R. or some other drug reference and writing down pertinent data on a 3x5 card for future reference when I could simply refer to the same books at any time to find the same information. Hence, I never made any drug cards. At our final evaluation for the end of the semester we were told to come to the office for the evaluation and bring all our cards for the review. At my appointed time, I arrived without any medication cards.

My evaluation was going quite well until she asked for the cards. I was forced to say that I didn't have any and gave her my reasoning for not making the cards. Once again, I saw that look of frustration on her face, but she didn't let into me, but rather stated that she knew I was competent and knew my medications. She witnessed my management of drugs and knowledge of their use many times during the semester. She felt comfortable that I was capable. Again, she asked me to never mention this to anyone and it would stay a secret, (until now). She helped me get my teaching position and I was thankful she did, because if not for that challenge, I might not have finished the program due to boredom.

Continuing Education in Life

My second semester I had an instructor from "Hell" (as described by my upper classmen). Her name was Beverly and she was tough! At our first conference, she asked what I expected from the coming semester. I told her that I wanted to obtain a grade of "A" in the practical portion and at least a "C" in academics. She promptly informed me that she considered an "A" as being perfect, something she rarely ever gave a student. I looked her square in the eye and told her that she was looking at her next "A" and that I would do whatever it took to get the grade. I could tell she had no confidence in my ability to fulfill that goal. Suffice to say, I did achieve that goal and even surpassed my goal for the academic grade. I made the Dean's list that semester which was the first time in my entire academic career that I accomplished that feat.

My third semester presented a bigger challenge, primarily from fellow instructors who previously took issue with my status as an instructor and student within the same department. My next instructor was one of the instructors who had made the biggest stink over my position. She made it clear that she was gunning for me. This semester would prove to be way too dangerous for me to stay in the program, so I made the decision not return to school after the summer break. Instead I chose to move to Big Bear Lake, California to help Eli open a gun shop. As it turned out, Eli never seemed to have real motivation to get the gun shop up and running and by Christmas of 1975, I realized I was wasting my time.

Just before the holiday, I paid my old college a visit to wish friends there a Merry Christmas and to explore options for re-entering the program. To my delight, the instructor who had posed problems the semester before had been placed on leave for a breakdown. She was no longer an obstacle to my success and I was clear of her threats. There were several new replacement instructors that semester. I successfully finished the third semester and then proceeded to the last phase of training where I continued to teach the paramedic program. I completed the fourth semester without any major incident.

Next, came the state boards' grueling exam. I spent two days locked behind closed doors. The exam was timed to generally allow you about 90 seconds to answer each question. There wasn't any time to waste. It was almost impossible to take a bathroom break. The results wouldn't be available for at least two months. Everyone in my class received their results by the two-month deadline except me. It was against the rules but I finally called the state board to inquire under the guise that I was taking a position overseas and needed to know right now if I passed. The voice on the other end of the phone said: "yes you passed" and explained my address was incorrect. Despite what she said, I hung up the phone and felt a state of panic come over me, thinking that maybe I had failed. I was a nervous wreck until I finally received the documents in the mail two weeks later.

Nurses Revolt!

My years in the military was the only time in my life that I felt I had real value as a human being until it carried over into my nursing career. I was good at my job but I had a very bad habit of becoming emotionally involved with my patients. Over time this trait would prove to be devastating to my psyche. The very thing that made me good at my job was the same thing that would drive me to several failed suicide attempts. I now know the reason I failed was because it wasn't meant to be. In the grand scheme of life, I still had something to learn about myself and the world around me.

During this time, I was employed at a Medical Center in Palm Desert, California. The hospital acquired the services of a Cardiac Surgeon with plans to start an Open-Heart program. The hospital didn't have enough staff to cover a brand-new unit yet; especially one that requires specialty nurses for the Intensive Care unit. To solve this dilemma the staff on my unit were informed that we would float to the new C.C.U. I was working in a step-down unit designed to treat patients with M.I. that were ready to be transferred out of the Critical Care area, but who still had a high probability to re-infarct. My unit was equipped with telemetry for monitoring the heart activity of our patients, but we were by no means qualified to be Critical Care Nurses.

Everyone on the unit was upset about the possibility of being placed in an area where we weren't qualified to work. We were concerned for the safety of the patients. Our concern didn't seem to affect the hospital Administration one bit. They continued to insist that we work both units. I hired a labor attorney, telling the staff I found a benefactor who supported our position and volunteered to pay the legal fees (although I paid the fees up front). I did this simply because I knew the staff couldn't pay and was afraid they might not be willing to stand up for what they believed to be true.

Our attorney told us that under the Nurse Practice Act of the State of California, it was very clear that if we felt we were not qualified to work in a specialty area, we were obligated to refuse the assignment or risk the loss of our license to practice (had any mistakes been made.) We presented it to the management team and they were less than receptive. They eventually came around to our way of thinking when they realized we were going to walk if they forced the issue. They did back down, but not before they got their revenge on me for being the ringleader of the revolt.

During this time, I requested a transfer to the Emergency Room with the intent of training as an E.R. nurse. One night, during the problem period, I get a phone call at home from the Manager of the E.R. telling me to come in and meet with her tonight at mid-night, as she was working the night shift that week. I arrived 15 minutes early and assumed this might impress her but it was a waste of time. She called me in to pressure me into distancing myself from the group of nurses with whom I worked (those who were supporting the revolt). She told me flat out that if I wanted to transfer to her department I could but only if I had no further association with the group and if I was willing to never discuss the matter again. I proceeded to tell her what she could do with her transfer, making it clear that I didn't respond well to threats or intimidation.

It just so happened that the assistant Director of Nursing at the time was a very good friend of mine. She took offense at what the hospital was doing to me and the staff on my unit. Furthermore, she had just been offered the Director of Nursing position at a hospital in Las Vegas, Nevada. She offered me a position at this new facility and I felt the time was right for a move. My unit stuck together and we did win out in the end. The Administration relented and finally retreated from their original position. They hired qualified nurses from a registry in Los Angeles.

Looking back, I realize it was fortuitous timing for me to make the move because, not only was I able to continue my work as a R.N., but I would soon be exposed to the American Society of Magicians and that affiliation would change my life...again.

As chaotic and stressful as my nursing career began, I served many communities throughout the country for four decades and encountered thousands of souls. Although I feel my life was well spent, I still had a hole in my soul when I'd think about how I wasn't wanted when I entered this world.

Clowning Around Vegas

A little background about a childhood fantasy: One day when we were kids sitting around, we discussed what we wanted to do for a living. When it was my turn, I said that my first choice was to be a clown in the circus. They laughed at me, but then asked the question; "why" had I never tried and, honestly, I was wondering myself.

One day in 1975, while reading the Palm Springs newspaper, I saw an ad for open auditions with the Ringling Brothers Circus. I called and set an appointment for the tryouts. I walked in to the auditions cold turkey with no background or skills and subsequently made a complete ass of myself. However, I was not to be deterred from my goal and continued with the help of a retired make-up artist from Paramount Studios. I traveled to Hollywood to find some research books on the art of clowning and its history. I also found books on juggling, unicycle, balloon art and began teaching myself what I needed to know to be a clown.

In the very beginning I was so bad at clowning that I only booked jobs for special needs groups and senior citizen retirement homes. I provided my services free of charge so if I wasn't funny or entertaining they really couldn't complain. I used this time to smooth out the rough edges and develop my skills. I did this concurrently at the start of my Nursing career and continued working both fields for about a year until certain events at the hospital happened and changed the direction of my life once more.

I met a man named Earl who had been a clown with Ringling Brothers. He retired to start his own clown business for private parties and affairs. He took me under his wing and began to teach me all the things I was sorely lacking as a clown. Then he booked jobs for me at local functions. While starting my clowning career I still worked in healthcare. It made for a nice change switching from one job to the other. It also gave me a chance to experience some of the most exciting times in my life. I performed for Jerry Lewis at his annual telethon, worked a convention for Kentucky Fried Chicken, and performed for the Sahara Hotel, Hilton Hotel and many others.

The high point of my time in Vegas was when Earl submitted me to the McDonalds Corporation to be a regional Ronald McDonald. They accepted me and I started my first gig as Ronald around 1981- 1982 at Hell Dorado Days in Las Vegas. I had a few minutes of fame when I was interviewed by the local T.V. station during the parade down the strip in Vegas.

It was terrific spending time as the most recognized face in the world. Image was so important to the company that I was never allowed to drive myself to a performance as Ronald. They always sent a limo for me. (I later discovered that I couldn't drive as a matter of safety. Ronald driving a car was too dangerous because he is so recognizable that it distracts other drivers.) One more perk I earned was I could eat all the free food I wanted from McDonalds. Not a bad perk when you are also being paid $150 for one hour of work to wave at the crowds that line the street.

Another high point in my clowning career was a promotional gig I worked at a mall in Vegas for Red Skelton. It was rumored that he did a painting of my clown character. I don't know if there is any truth to the story but I was told that by the owner of the art gallery that displayed Red's works.

I named my clown character "Jasper" for two reasons: First, when I was young Jo often referred to me "Jasper Do Do". Secondly, Jasper is the modem day equivalent of the name Gaspar. Traditionally, Gaspar was believed to be the name of one of the three wise men to visit the Christ child in the manger. I took this as a sign that I was meant to be called Jasper the Clown.

(More than twenty years later, Jasper is still alive but now I only do charity work because I find getting paid takes away the enjoyment for me when performing as a clown.)

A Musical Side Show

My Ronald McDonald career ended when I took to the road again. This time as a Road Manager for a rock and roll band that my cousin, Margo started in New Orleans, featuring an Elvis impersonator. After two years in Vegas I called my cousin in New Orleans and asked her if she would like me to try and book a performance for the band in Vegas. She agreed even though I didn't have a clue how to get jobs for a band. I went to see one of the Entertainment Directors at the Sahara Hotel and walked out with a gig for the band. I immediately called Margo with the good news. Within a month my apartment was filled with nine musicians and a half a dozen roadies.

During this time, I was still working as a Critical Care Nurse at a hospital in Las Vegas. Within one week of the bands arrival I turned in my letter of resignation to the hospital and traveled as a road manager for the band. Next, we headed for Reno for a show at the Reno Sahara. If I had known what I was doing I might have recognized early on that musicians are a real pain. This group could never agree on anything without a fight. I found them a great job working for a hotel chain in California but they turned the offer down, claiming they were home sick. (Then why choose a profession that you know will keep you on the road all the time, I thought?)

The band and I parted ways after finishing a gig in Florida. I packed and drove straight to California in a little over 24 hours. I was glad to be back home again. Eventually, I returned to Vegas, resumed my job as an R.N. at the same hospital and continued my Clowning career until I met a man who made me an offer I couldn't refuse. My new position was with a security firm that protected a Nevada test site but I also hoped to secure a contract to provide Infirmary services at the same location. I felt I would be an asset if they were awarded the contract, so I left the hospital and hung up my clown suit to start my new career as a Security Officer.

Security Job

The first 6 months I sat in an office building at the Las Vegas airport waiting for the government to complete my security clearance. (I can't discuss my duties because there may still be a time limit in effect for revealing what we did and where we did it). I spent four days a week, working 18-hour shifts with six hours off in-between. Towards the end of my time as a security guard at the test site, I worked at the farthest outpost that we manned, about twenty-five miles out in the middle of the Nevada desert.

After the next six months, word came down that the Boss received instructions from corporate to promote four men to the rank of sergeant. The pool of candidates consisted of eight men so right up front we all realized that four guys were going to be disappointed. I was the only one with a college degree and with experience in a leadership role. I assumed I would be one of the four promoted. Wrong!

Four candidates were Caucasian and four African-American. Due to a government requirement, they passed over me to comply with some federal employment law. I was very unhappy and voiced my objections to my boss only to hear him say: "Jim, you are right for the job but I have no choice in this matter". I decided to quit because I felt I had been given the shaft only because (this time) I was the wrong color. Once again, life was telling me that I wasn't worthy.

However, before I left that position I had an unplanned flight back to Vegas from the test site due to a family emergency. My watch sergeant called and said to expect a driver shortly and that upon his arrival I was to return to the duty section. I was concerned why I was being called in because this was during the friction caused by the promotion mishap. Upon arrival, I reported to the duty sergeant and was informed that my Uncle had died and that transportation had been arranged from the test site to San Diego.

Las Vegas 1981

Losing an Uncle and a Father

Because of the significant impact it had on my life, I need to provide more detail surrounding my uncle's murder at the hands of his brother. It wouldn't be till I arrived that I found out why I wasn't given any explanation about how he had died. I learned that Herb, my ex-father, was the person who killed him. Herb was an alcoholic. Around 1982, he entered a treatment program at the V.A. and was placed on Antabuse. (This compound is designed to make you violently ill if you consume alcohol while taking it.) Unknown to most people, one to two percent of individuals using this drug have a psychotic break if they consume alcohol concurrently. Herb was one of those individuals. During a failed attempt at sobriety he consumed both alcohol and Antabuse. He and his brother Donald had an argument that ended with Herb stabbing Donald to death. Herb unsuccessfully tried to commit suicide by putting his head in the oven and turning on the gas and then by cutting his wrist. He was taken into police custody.

I had to fly out of Vegas so quickly, I didn't have time to pack so I arrived in San Diego with only the clothes on my back. My grandmother immediately produced clothes for me to wear but they belonged to my deceased uncle and I just didn't feel comfortable wearing them. At the funeral, I heard one guest whisper: "who is the man who looks like Donald? Is that his son?" Having Herb murder my uncle and attempt suicide was devastating enough but then hearing people think I was Donald's son only compounded my heartache. This incident painfully reminded me that I started life unwanted and here I once again was feeling like I was on the outside looking in.

After the service, I excused myself, got in my uncle's car and drove down to the beach in Del Mar where he had lived. I found a bar on the beach with the full intention of getting sloppy drunk, however, I failed at the effort. A couple hours later I went to see a priest to see if he could relieve all the pain I was feeling. I felt shame for Herb and for myself. I didn't have much self-esteem and this event made everything worse. Somehow, I felt responsible for what had happened (probably a trained response since I was raised to always be at fault somehow). Thankfully, I now know my thinking was incorrect at the time. I have since learned that we are the product of all the occurrences of our lives and the influence they have on us. I know I was not responsible for Donald's death.

Herb was eventually placed in a mental health hospital for the next five years. Just before his release I had the opportunity to meet with Herb at the hospital and he made a request that I was unable to fulfill. He said that he needed someone to take responsibility for him to be released and asked me if I would be that person. I know I was in shock for a while but finally realized this wasn't something I could do, not because I held a grudge for his actions but rather out of fear. I wasn't sure I could trust him not to repeat his actions in the future.

Herb was disappointed but he didn't hold it against me. My Grandmother took on this burden. In all fairness to Herb (and without trying to forgive his horrific actions), he did turn his life around. Years later he graduated from National University with a B.S. and a Master's Degree in Psychology. He put his education to good use as a Chemical Dependency Counselor in the Long Beach area. I had contact with him a few times while I lived in in San Pedro, just 15 minutes from where he lived. Somehow, our relationship was never the same as before but we were able to build a new one based on my respect for what Herb had done with his life after the fact. I'm very proud of his turn around and his dedication to helping other people with a problem he knows all too well.

It didn't occur to me at the time, but Herb's example showed me how to turn my own life around even though I was too blind and confused at the time to realize it. It was easier to just avoid my own personal and emotional issues and I did. I lost track of Herb in 1998 after my wife and I moved to northern California. I think it's safe to assume he is still in Long Beach working with fellow alcoholics and hopefully doing some good. Perhaps, it's atonement for his actions in his past.

Jobs and More Jobs

As I was beginning my nursing career, I reflected on the many other interesting jobs I was privileged to hold. At age 16, I took a job as a "pool boy" with a gentleman who owned a pool service company. This job stands out for two reasons. First, the job required a driver so the owner had to teach me to drive a stick shift before I could work for him. The second reason is because I learned what it's like to be laid off from a job I truly enjoyed. Several months after I started working, the boss hired a fulltime worker who was a married man with a family. Apparently, he needed more than part-time help.

The boss also took it on himself to find me a new job. The day I was laid off he proceeded to walk with me to a local coffee shop where he introduced me to the owner. The new employer gave me an apron, showed me the washing station and put me to work as a dishwasher. (I had decided years before that I would never work at a job like this.) I lasted twenty minutes, took off the apron and handed it to the owner. I thanked him for the opportunity, but said that I wasn't interested in being a dishwasher.

Less than a week later I found a better job in Palm Springs working for the local car dealership. The job paid better and was more fun. I was responsible for maintaining cars in the used car lot. Eventually, I was allowed to transport cars to and from Los Angeles. Ironically, a week later the pool service owner called and asked me to come back because his full-time family man wasn't doing as much work as I did part-time. I enjoyed telling him "no" and learned that a loyal employer is something of a myth. (We like to think that all employers care about us but some are primarily concerned with their bottom line.)

During my time in college I had some of the best jobs. I was an investigator for the Veterans Administration at the college I attended. Seems quite a few of my fellow-veterans were using their G.I. Bill for college but never attended class. Some signed up only to get the monthly V.A. check. My job was to find those who received benefits but not attending classes. I busted quite a few guys for defrauding the V.A. and saved taxpayers thousands of dollars, so it was a job well done.

Most Bizarre Job

Welcome to the craziest job I had while attending college. I responded to an ad on the student info board seeking a live-in nursing student. My job was to control the dietary plan of a client. The man lived in a country club in the Mojave Desert near Palm Springs, California. He was a very wealthy, retired Industrialist from the east. He had a big problem with self-control when it came to food and he assumed that a nursing student could keep track of his diet and make sure he wasn't eating things he shouldn't. I frequently found cookies and other assorted candy wrappers under his bed or stuffed under his pillow

The job paid a fair wage and came with room and board. My room was at the back of his 4000-square foot home near the laundry room. Everything was going fine until late one night when I was awakened by a strange noise outside my room. After investigating I discovered that the washing machine and dryer next to my bedroom wall was the source. Both machines were filled with golf balls being washed and dried. This alone is strange enough but it was also two o'clock in the morning.

I went into the house and found the kitchen in total disarray. Food items from the opened cupboards had been placed in the sink with running water flowing over onto the floor. When I reached the living room, I found all his video recording equipment set up complete with lights as though he was making a full-length movie.

I decided that I should find him and see if he was all right. He was nowhere to be found so I expanded my search to the outside yard area. His car was on the front lawn but there was no sight of him. I felt like I might be in over my head and decided to get out of Dodge as soon as possible. My car was parked on the street in front of the house and had been hit by another car and it didn't take long to find out who hit me! So, I ended another job but none had such a bizarre ending as this one.

Lesson Learned from Molestation

At age twelve, I was exposed to the world of sex when I was molested. Herb and a friend decided to try an opportunity selling a product to coat surfaces that prevents them from being scuffed or marred. The master plan was to get local high schools interested in using it on football helmets. (The business venture eventually failed.)

One Saturday afternoon Herb and I went to his partner's house to demonstrate the product. We spent the day cleaning an entire team's helmets and then applying the compound. We worked hard most of the day and I recall that it was fun. Somehow, I ended up spending the night, and sure enough, Herb's partner introduced me to sex. Even though it <u>must</u> be considered molestation, I find it most interesting that I never felt traumatized by the experience, rather I was intrigued by the encounter. However, I did feel like I had done something wrong and decided to keep this secret from my parents (and the world). I wanted to avoid dealing with what I knew would be a calamity of astronomical proportions if they knew.

My inner self was never that satisfied to begin with so this made it easier for me to step into the world of sex for money. After experiencing sex (for free), I instinctively knew this was an area of great earning potential. (Even today, sex is one of the most productive ways to earn money with over a billion dollars a year in profits.)

I've kept this secret for more than forty years but I reveal it now to show people that humans have a greater capacity for survival than they give themselves credit for. I firmly believe that God can use these things to make us stronger. I'm living proof that people can survive and even prosper with the right perspective of not taking life so serious. It would be many years though before I learned this lesson.

I was hurt by many things in this life but sex wasn't one of those. Perhaps that experience should have produced a failure, but it didn't. In spite of it, I learned to succeed regardless of the obstacles placed in my way. Innate ability resides in all of us if we take the time to look inside and pay attention to our higher selves' voices when they speak to us.

A Mexican Marriage and Divorce

In 1974, I returned home to learn that my mom, Jo, had hired a high school age housekeeper named Betty. When I first entered the house, I saw a young lady cleaning the oven with her buttocks sticking up in the air! There was an immediate attraction. Two weeks later we took a trip to Mexico with the intent of getting married as quickly as possible. (I think I might have married an American Mexican girl who did not speak Spanish!)

I'm not certain if we were married because the entire process was in a language I didn't speak. I was suspicious of the entire event because we were shuffled around for half a day and asked for money at every moment in the process!

We stood before a man in robes who looked like a judge, but for all I know he could have been a janitor on his lunch break looking to earn a few extra pesos. It doesn't really matter if he was a judge or not because within two months our relationship was over.

I went to Tijuana, Mexico and paid an attorney to complete my divorce. I didn't even need her signature on the forms to make it official. That was the beginning and end of my first encounter with marriage. It would be nearly fourteen years before I would commit to a serious relationship that resulted in marriage.

Longing for My Comrades

I continued to try my luck at different types of nursing positions. I worked in Intensive Care then moved to Emergency Care and even did a stint as a camp nurse for United Cerebral Palsy. I also worked as a prison nurse in Las Vegas and eventually was offered a job at Folsom State Prison, a position which I turned down on the day I arrived for my employment physical.

As I was escorted to the infirmary through the exercise yard, I found myself surrounded by over 500 inmates, all just standing around. Somehow, I wasn't very impressed with the security, so I decided to forgo the position and very soon afterwards chose to re-enter the military instead.

It had been twelve years since I left the Air Force. I decided to go back to the life I enjoyed the most. Whereas, most people probably hate the structure of the military, I thrived on it and I was never happier than my time in the service. However, I knew from my experiences that it's impossible to go back in life or to recapture a moment in time. When you try to go back to a life you once had, it's never quite the same. Knowing this, I decided to choose a different branch of the service this time: The United States Navy. I even chose Fire Control, a new field of study.

Fire Control is the operator of the weapons systems on board a Navy vessel. I received training in beginning and advanced electronic computer systems and guidance for the weapon system using Radar. I was quite the sailor with above average evaluations and rapid advancement. I was in the top of my classes during the training phase. This fact alone would make my future with the Navy a very difficult experience as I'll explain.

Honorary Citizen of the Day in Chicago

A moment of fame I had during my tenure with the Navy was being part of the Saturday Scholars Program. The Navy started a program to assist inner city children with tutoring on the weekends. The goal was to help them progress at a more even pace with their contemporaries in the suburbs. I had the privilege to tutor two children in Math and English. Both were very bright kids and learned quickly after someone (me) showed an interest in them.

We taught classes at a school across the street from Rev. Jesse Jackson's Rainbow Coalition Headquarters. When the assignment was complete, my fellow sailors and I were honored with Honorary Citizens of the Day for the city of Chicago, accompanied with proclamations of gratitude. I wonder what became of my two students. I expect they did well in life, no matter the circumstance, because they were both very bright and motivated young children.

After I completed my electronics training at the naval station in Chicago at Great Lakes Naval Station I was in route to San Diego for advanced training. Along the way, I had to choose if I was going home with my leave time or to Sacramento to work at the summer camp I worked the year before. At the very last minute I decided to go home. It just so happened that my parents were planning to be in Las Vegas for the annual Surplus Buyers trade show that Eli attended every year. Little did I know that the decision to meet them in Vegas would prove to be the most important one I ever made.

Meeting Rona

My first night in Las Vegas, I was introduced to a beautiful woman named Rona. She would eventually become my wife, best friend and savior. I had plans that night but it didn't include a blind date (that's what Rona was)! When we first met we blew each other off as quickly as possible and went our separate ways. Two days later we met again at a reception. Rona was wearing a red dress and in my eyes, she was definitely hot! She invited herself to visit the family ranch and I'm very glad that she took that initiative because a few weeks later I fell madly in love with someone for the first time in my life. I felt emotion inside like nothing I had ever experienced before. To say I was in heaven was to put it mildly. I knew then that I had truly never known what it felt like to love another human being. That was the greatest experience of my entire life.

We married on October 31, 1987 and Yes...we married on Halloween! It was a secret wedding with only a best man and a maid of honor. The reason for the secrecy was simply because her parents hadn't warmed up to me yet and we were afraid they wouldn't approve. We kept it a secret until late November when we told her family that we planned to get married on the 31st of December for tax purposes. Her family bought it hook line and sinker but unfortunately, all didn't go according to plan.

My mother, Jo, disrupted our plans simply because she objected to me inviting Herb. As you know, Herb had been my primary father from age 5 years until I was nearly fourteen and I wanted him there. Jo threw a fit and refused to attend. She even returned all our wedding gifts that had been sent to her home. Some wedding well-wishers were afraid to send their gifts directly to Rona and I for fear Jo might find out and it would cause big rifts in their relationships with her.

Nevertheless, the day still turned out to be one of the high points in my life. Rona was so beautiful that day as she walked down the aisle. On this, our second wedding day, our daughter, Lindy, stood up with Rona as maid of honor. She was tickled pink to be a part of the process.

When Lindy was much older, we told her the truth about our weddings. It has worked out very well for us: each year I plan an anniversary day on the 31st of October and Rona makes plans on her anniversary, the 31st off December! This is the perfect sequel to the rest of my life for when I married Rona, I feel my life began all over again.

My Daughter Lindy

I absolutely received a double bonus when I married Rona. First, I got a wife most men would die for and secondly, I was so very fortunate to acquire a daughter at the same time. Her name is Lindy Nicole and she is the apple of my eye. I thank God, every day for the privilege to be her Father.

In the first 17 years of our happy life together, Lindy's biological Father contacted her one time. He made a gigantic error when he contacted her to wish her happy birthday by getting the year and her age wrong. She was extremely upset that he wasn't aware of her correct age. Lindy asked and we granted permission for her to write a response to him. I never got to read Lindy's letter but Rona did and she told me it basically stated that she had found a man who knew how to treat her like a daughter and she had no need for him to be in her life. I found it very rewarding to hear my daughter speak so highly of me. It temporarily lifted my low self-esteem, having the knowledge that someone really did like me and wanted me in their life.

Lindy is one of the most intelligent people I have come across even in all of my travels. She has a gift for language and an uncanny ability to read people. When Lindy was 12 or 13 years old she took it upon herself to write a letter to the Editor of the local newspaper. The topic of her letter was homosexual students in the grade school system. The focus of the letter was to support all children regardless of their sexual preference and to express her belief that to discriminate against them was wrong on any level. You can imagine our surprise when we received a phone call from the Editor requesting our permission to print the article. He was equally surprised when he found out the age of the writer. He couldn't believe that a child as young as Lindy could have the level of insight and understanding of life that she held.

Inspired by Lindy

Believe it or not, because of Lindy's inspiration I had the opportunity to publish some technical writing in a national publication. That work which now bears my name is only there because of my daughter. Lindy has been my personal editor since I became her Father. She was only 13 years old when she cleaned up my article for publication. How amazing to have such a command of the English language at such an early age. Whenever I find myself in need of editing I turn to her because she is a natural.

Lindy completed college at the University of Oregon with a degree in Romance Languages. She is amusing to watch in the public arena when she encounters people of Latin or Hispanic descent. They look at her and see a 5 foot 10 inch, blonde hair, blue eyed female who can converse or verbally lambaste them in their native language. She is currently working in an executive computer position for a staffing agency.

Lindy makes me very proud to know she is making her mark in life by helping other people find gainful employment. She married her childhood sweetheart, have two beautiful children and reside in Portland, Oregon.

Rona and I vs the U.S. Navy

Rona and I faced the first major obstacle in our marriage with the U.S. Navy. Shortly after our wedding, I received deployment orders to spend four years in Japan. Rona told me flat out that she couldn't be a Navy wife if I would be gone all the time. The only solution I could think of was to leave the Navy. Now this might seem like an easy task, but it wasn't. First, I hired an attorney to represent me in my fight to be released. After he reviewed the facts, he told me it wouldn't be a problem to request an early release. He said there were several Naval regulations that applied to my case and all I had to do was complete some forms and wait to be released. I didn't figure into the equation that as an excellent sailor, the Navy might not want to release me.

I will never forget the day when the Master Chief of the school called me into his office to ask why he had been served with legal documents and, furthermore, why hadn't I come to him first. I explained the situation but he tried to dissuade me. Instead, he said I was a good sailor and that we could find a way to work this out.

One year and $4000 later I was still in the Navy and stationed at Long Beach Naval Station aboard the Battleship New Jersey. Apparently, the Navy had hoped that by stationing me at Long Beach, I might change my mind but, alas, I was still determined.

When those attempts failed, I had to take drastic measures to accomplish my goal after I received orders for New Jersey. As I departed San Diego Naval Station, I made the choice to get out no matter what the cost.

I headed to a family cabin at Lake Big Bear and proceeded to go A.W.O.L. (absent without leave). A friend supplied some marijuana and I spent the next 17 days at the cabin...paranoid and alone.

After my absence, I decided to report for duty in dress uniform to the Watch Commander aboard the New Jersey. I saluted the flag and requested permission to come aboard and approached the Officer of the Day. I reported that I was 17 days A.W.O.L. and that I had been smoking marijuana. This immediately threw the Officer of the Day into a tailspin. He had no idea what to do with me.

He called the Shore Patrol and the next thing I knew I was escorted below deck to the Shore Patrol office. They sat me down and said they would get back to me as soon as they knew what to do with me. An hour later the Petty Officer who escorted me returns and tells me to go home and report to my workstation at 0700 the next morning.

Rona was very surprised to see me that evening. When I left the house that morning, she was certain I wouldn't be home any time soon. I was sure I had broken the rules and would be punished. Before long I was sent back to San Diego to stand charges.

I received a reduction in rate and lost one half a month's pay, times 45 days for 45 days of jail time. Fortunately, I remained a squared away sailor and was released after 21 days of confinement. My early release might have had something to do with the base inspection. I stood that weekend with the Base

Commander and I was pulled out of the ranks as an example of what a good sailor should look like right down to the spit shine on my boots. Regardless of the reason, I was released to civilian life and no worse for wear.

My drive home was one of the most enjoyable I have ever experienced. My Naval career was over. The only responsibility that lay ahead of me now was married life. The logical choice I made for employment was to re-enter the Nursing profession.

Rona's Health Scare

Just prior to my release from the Navy, I got the scare of my life when I learned that the Red Cross was trying to reach me. The message said that a doctor from San Pedro, California, (our hometown) was trying to reach me. I immediately called to discover that my wife may have a tumor in her right kidney. The Navy agreed to release me on emergency leave. It turned out that she didn't have a tumor, rather an aberrant blood vessel to the capsule of her right Kidney that had ruptured and bled 800cc into the space behind her kidney.

We felt lucky that we dodged the bullet but about six months after she fully recovered, she found a lump in her breast. After testing, it turned out that she was positive for two forms of cancer in one breast that required surgery. (Rona is quite a woman considering she has had surgery more than twenty times in her life.) After breast surgery, she needed mandatory chemotherapy and radiation therapy. This process would take most of the next year to complete.

Midway through the process I was laid off at the hospital which was unsettling since I had to work for matters of financial practicality. Not to worry, I secured a new position before the ink dried on my final paycheck. Most of all, I'm just thankful that I didn't lose the most important person in my life.

The whole experience taught me a great deal about how the system of healthcare works....and fails. When a woman is given this type of diagnosis, all attention shifts to her and the husband is sadly forgotten. Granted the husband isn't facing death but he faces the possibility of losing his mate and in my case, the loss of my soul mate. I truly don't know what I would have done if I had lost Rona. I may have been able to carry on but I really don't know.

Fortunately, the hospital that had laid me off gave me two months' severance pay which bought us some time to decide what to do. Our first choice was to take a long-awaited vacation. We rented a R.V. and drove to Vegas, then the Kern River where we experienced white water rafting for the first time. It was one of the best times we shared as husband and wife. Too bad it couldn't have lasted longer.

After the trip, we returned to San Pedro for Rona to complete her radiation therapy. Thank God and all the Saints that Rona is a cancer survivor some 15 years now. She did develop Diabetes however but remains cancer free and I intend to keep it that way...with a lot of prayers.

My Health Scare

Rona had just finished her treatments for breast cancer when we were at a restaurant for lunch when I suddenly dropped dead. I had just finished eating and took a drink when suddenly I felt the worst pain I ever felt, right under my sternum. I looked in Rona's eyes and was unable to speak except to say goodbye. I fell to the floor, according to Rona, and no one could find a pulse anywhere. I stopped breathing for several minutes but then like a light bulb being turned on, I woke up. I was on the floor looking at pieces of food people had dropped and wondered what the heck happened. By then the ambulance arrived and I watched the scope to see what my heart rhythm looked like.

I decided it wasn't looking too bad so I told the paramedics to leave me alone that I was alright and would go home to rest. I didn't improve over the next few days so Rona took me in to see my doctor. I'll never forget his words when he walked into the exam room. He took one look at me and asked Rona: "does he look this gray all the time?" We spent the next six years trying to get a diagnosis for what had occurred. Turns out I have a problem with my vagus nerve. I have been fortunate that all repeating episodes were never as severe as the very first time. I've learned to tolerate the condition quite well.

Eli's Death and Jo's New Mate

Around this same time, Eli, my mother's 4th husband died. After a surgery and during his post-op recovery period, developed a blood clot and died instantly. I felt strange going to his funeral dressed in my Navy whites because no one knew who I was. The Rabbi even referred to me as the man with Jo. Of course, Eli's death meant that Jo would be looking for a new mate and she found one less than three months after we buried Eli.

Jo's new mate was named Jack. We have never met and all things considered, I don't care if we do. Many years have gone by and Jo has made no effort to make contact even though I have tried several times. She has taken several trips to Montana to be with his family and never stops to visit even though it's on the way. My Grandparents from Herb have stopped a few times...until a few years ago when they stopped coming too. I know they felt awkward visiting me while still maintaining their relationship with Jo and Jack. I'm sorry not to see them anymore but I respect their choice, no matter what.

Fleeting Family

The only other close family member I currently have is my Mother-in Law. Her name is Helen and she is quite remarkable. She moved from the coal mines of West Virginia to California with her husband Larry. In less than 20 years, they built an empire of more than ten locations providing second-hand clothing and similar items for people who couldn't afford to shop at fancy malls and expensive stores. We lost Larry in the early 1990's and he is still missed today as much as ever. He was truly a self-made man with great insight and a head for math like no one I have ever met. Helen is one of the most experienced world travelers that I have ever known. She has a natural talent for finding just the right antique or household item anyone might want. If there is a bargain to be found, Helen will find it and if you aren't careful she might get it for a dime!

We haven't talked to my wife's sister Rene, her spouse and son in years. Rene left the state under the cover of darkness, escaping a warrant issued in San Diego for her arrest after she stole my father-in-law's entire (and sizeable) estate. I know she thinks she got away with the crime but her time will come, if not this life, then the next. I mention this side of the family to be fair. My brother-in-law is a nice enough guy but I have little respect for a man who is devoid of backbone and the necessary grit to stand up for himself OR what is right. My nephew leaves a lot to be desired however, I wish them no harm. I hope life treats them fair and they maintain good health.

We have more family, but don't live close enough for regular visits.

Searching and Finding Birth Family

Now to expose the final secret of my life and it's quite juicy. Shortly, after Lindy graduated from the university, Rona suggested that we move from the Los Angeles area into a more wholesome environment. We moved to Siskiyou County, California, in the shadow of Mount Shasta; a 14,000-foot volcanic peak located off Interstate 5 and just south of the Oregon border. It is God's country. We love it here and have never been more happy and relaxed.

Just after we moved, I received a letter from my cousin Frances in New Orleans stating that she would like to try to find my biological parents and wanted to know if I objected. My responded that I had no problem with her searching even though I had unsuccessfully tried many years earlier. I didn't believe she would have any more success than I because in California, documents are sealed and it takes an "act of Congress" to open those records. I didn't realize what Frances could do in the computer age and she began her search. She eventually contacted a woman in the San Diego area who was willing to do some leg work.

After a year or so, I received a letter from Frances with the results. She found my biological Mother and her name is Mercedes. She was rather difficult to locate because she lived in a San Diego skilled nursing facility. She also found reference to my Grandmother's death records for the county. She had died just a few years prior at age 84. I don't know why but it felt strange finding out that I had a real Grandmother that lived in San Diego my whole life.

It would be a trigger that started my final slide into acute depression on a level I had never experienced before. It was a relief to learn the truth about my beginnings, however, it also turned out to be a nightmare, primarily because I already lacked self-esteem and a sense of self-worth.

Son of a Rapist

Prior to meeting my birth mother, I spoke to a family member who explained the shocking story of how I came to be: Sometime in December of 1950, a U.S. Marine (stationed at Camp Pendleton, California) was stalking Mercy. He followed her out of the base Bowling Alley one dark night and grabbed her against her will.

He took her to a secluded beach and used four point restraints before brutally beating her to within an inch of her life. His dirty work wasn't finished yet as he proceeded to viciously rape her several times and leave her for dead. This is the night that I was conceived and later born the son of a helpless victim and despicable rapist.

Mercy spent many years attempting to heal but never fully recovered. She was beaten on the right side of her face so bad that she had her cheekbone removed and multiple surgeries to follow. It's amazing that she and I both survived. Unfortunately, she was not capable of caring for me and I was placed for adoption.

Meeting Mercy and Birth Family

My most memorable experience was the day we met, by the way, was Mother's Day. Mercedes (who likes to be called Mercy) was a short, elderly, very frail woman about 5 feet tall who weighed only 85 lbs. My wife Rona spent time getting to know her, while I was more intent on learning about family history and where I came from. (Due to the injuries Mercy suffered she couldn't handle complex subjects.)

I pressed for more answers about my family history. First, I viewed family photos that meant very little to me. My persistence to see something more significant than old photos of people I will never meet paid off. An English Tea Serving cart was brought out and my cousin Matthew opens the drawer used for utensils and linen. In it revealed a hand-written family tree from as early as the 1600's when an original family member left Northern Europe via Scotland for New England. Dates of births and deaths and who was who was written in pencil on satin. I can't describe what I felt emotionally when I read the first name, the year and the list of names that followed. It made me feel attached to something for the first time in my life. It was a bittersweet experience for me though, since I couldn't get past the fact that I was the result of such a horrific event.

After pictures, hugs and the promise of the cart we said farewell. Having seen the ravages of that brutal attack in person, somehow, I felt responsible and left with a tremendous amount of guilt. Mercy's right Zygomatic bone was removed as it was crushed from the beating she took, during the attack. She had dozens of surgeries that first year just to restore the damage this man committed. I take no pleasure and feel only shame knowing that one half of my DNA comes from such a sick animal.

My first visit with Mercy and birth family was the last encounter of any nature. It seems cousin Tim was worried that I was looking for a piece of the estate from a trust set up by my grandmother. I assured him during our first call to relax that I wasn't looking for money. All I wanted was to belong, but ultimately, the whole experience fell way short of my expectations.

More Questions than Answers

Why was I born under these circumstances? Why would God allow me to survive and put this poor soul, Mercy through such torture? Intellectually, I understand I wasn't responsible for what happened, but I just couldn't get past the facts of knowing how I was conceived. Tormenting thoughts continued to resonate through my mind over the next few years, in addition to the already existing list of things I found distasteful about myself. At this point I was still years away from finding all the right answers.

Rona says that I'm the spitting image of Mercy, but frankly I never saw it. I never felt completely comfortable around her even though she is the sweetest woman. I appreciate that she never placed any blame on me for what happened to her so many years ago.

I also learned that Mercy had a five-year-old son before I was born. Five years after I was born she had a daughter but because of her disabilities, the state of California took the child away from her. So somewhere in this world I have a brother and sister who don't know that I exist.

Mercy said that there was never an August 30th that passed (my birthday) that she didn't think about me and wondered what my life was like. She hoped and prayed that I had a good home and family.

I haven't had contact with Mercy or her spouse since. I tried hard to maintain contact and even invited Mercy to come spend time with Rona and I, but my cousin made sure that never happened. Eventually all contact ended. Rona is convinced that Mathew also must have been worried that I might try to put a claim on any kind of future inheritance even though I made it quite clear that all I wanted was the history of my origin and to obtain at least a partial knowledge of my family medical/health history.

It's been years now since I last heard from Mercy. She was 74 years old when we met over fifteen years ago, so I imagine that she has since passed. If Rona's theory is correct, it's not likely that we will ever hear from anyone else in my birth mother's family and I'm not holding my breath waiting.

My Life Made a Difference

The only positive I find from my birth status is that my head is screwed on correctly and that I've devoted my life to humanity. In one way or another I have always wanted to help people, if for no other reason than to be accepted. I have never intentionally hurt anyone.

I do wonder when I hear people talk about rape why everyone seems to agree that aborting a baby is acceptable. How many innocent souls have been put to death by abortion simply because they resulted from the effects of a rape? Could we have killed the person who may find a cure for Cancer or develop technology for travel to the far reaches of our universe? Who knows? I'm not going to try to change the way the world deals with the subject of rape or the actions people might take to resolve a rape pregnancy. I just want people to re-think their opinion on the topic with a bit more information and open-mindedness.

I do finally believe that I am a worthwhile human being and that my life had great value because I spent it helping people...not for personal gain, but rather out of a desire to be kind. I sometimes wonder if more people in this world tried to live like I do now, what a wonderful world this could be. I feel no hatred towards any human and would help anyone who asked-- regardless. So, in the end, I now know that I was way too hard on myself and took life way to serious but I have corrected that situation and now believe life is worth living.

Beginning of My Crash

In retrospect, I believe the end and, therefore, the beginning of my "new life" began shortly after my marriage to Rona. My wife is a true hero for tolerating my behavior for more than 16 years. I believe the "end" began with my release from the Navy when I broke my own honor code to get out of the Navy. That cost me dearly. Then Rona was diagnosed with cancer and I had a series of jobs lost to hospital downsizing.

Eventually we moved to northern California to escape the crowded city. In Yreka, California I had a few job-related problems. Small communities sometimes have a closed attitude towards newcomers. After several years of job disappointments, I made the transition to Traveling Nursing where I worked in the bay area for about two years at several hospitals as a traveling house Supervisor. I enjoyed the work, but grew tired of long distance travel and returned to a local hospital with possibly the worst management team I have ever encountered. Then in August of 2003, I could no longer hide my depressive disorder.

After my marriage, I started to slowly lose control of my depression and negative thoughts. My wife who was my rock, tried to push me into therapy for the first time but I wasn't ready to except help. A few months later I found myself deep in the depths of a huge black hole that was trying to swallow me up. I finally had enough of the pain and all those negative emotions that I was feeling. I concluded that the world would be a better place without me in it.

I've tried to end my life before but never had any luck. This occasion however, I decided to do it right. I bought some plastic hose about two inches in diameter and some duct tape and drove to the high desert by the Viet Nam War Memorial. I hooked the hose up to the back window and sealed the window so there would be no leakage. I started the engine, turned the radio on and sat there waiting to die! Apparently, God didn't want me to succeed that day because I sat there for over an hour and nothing happened. I took this as a sign, but didn't know what the sign was trying to tell me. I went home and kept the secret of my failed attempt. I returned to work and things seemed to be temporarily stable until August when I finally cracked, having a complete mental meltdown.

The Night this Nurse Needed Help

I went to work one evening like always and started my shift by getting a report from the off-going crew. My assignment was to care for five patients and all but one was independent. The shift should have been an easy night for me but I couldn't have been more wrong.

Don't ask me what happened to trigger everything but things went terribly wrong. Within ten minutes of hitting the floor I found myself standing outside a patient's room in tears. I just couldn't do my job. The worst feeling I had was knowing that I couldn't care for my patients. What I needed most was someone to care for me and I knew it wasn't safe for me to be at work.

Realizing I wasn't capable of caring for my patients, I knew I had to inform the Supervisor. This is where I encountered my first angel named Doris, my shift Supervisor. When she arrived on the unit I asked if we could speak elsewhere because I had something to discuss with her right now! She agreed and we went outside to the break area. As I began to tell her I wasn't capable of rendering care that night I did something I have never done before in my entire life...I confessed my problem to someone.

I stated how sick I was and that I needed help. She listened and never judged me reassuring me that she wouldn't use this information to feed the rumor mill at the hospital. She suggested I get help in the form of talk therapy. I agreed to find someone and hopefully find some solution to my depression. Doris was a true friend that night. It took me by surprise that she cared for my well-being as much as she did.

My second angel that night was Pat. She is also a Supervisor at the same hospital who I considered to be a close friend. Doris recommended I call Pat and discuss my situation so I did. She recommended the same thing as Doris so I called Sister Louise, a Catholic Nun with a Doctoral degree in Psychology. She is also the sister of Betty, our first friend in Yreka. (Ironically, she was in town to celebrate fifty years of service as a Nun.)

Sister Louise (my third angel) immediately came to my house to talk. Sadly, by the time she left, I found myself wondering if life was even worth the effort or if it would be easier for everyone if I just quit. Somehow, I found the strength to hang on and persevere.

I also had the support of my wife Rona whom I considered my fourth (guardian) angel. The next angel I encountered was my doctor, Rachael. I worship the ground she walks on. She has always been there for me as a well-qualified physician. I met her a few days after my meltdown. She agreed with my need for therapy, placed me on medication and confirmed my disability.

The hospital immediately sent me a letter stating that if I didn't return to work in a week I would be terminated. I called Rachael to let her know that her efforts to keep this information hidden from my employer had failed. The very hospital I worked for didn't have the time or the inclination to stand by me during the time I needed to recover (and return to work) although all my evaluations for this hospital were above average or better. I believe they were afraid I would apply for worker's compensation on the basis of stress and mental health problems but that wasn't the case. All I wanted was enough time to stop the pain, heal myself and return to work.

My Road to Restoration

Finally, I met Susan, my therapist and sixth angel. Initially I started therapy with someone else because she wasn't accepting new clients at the time. That encounter left me feeling like I knew more about psychiatric conditions than the therapist. Fortunately, Susan called me shortly after my first session with the other therapist and was willing to take me, starting the very next week.

After my first meeting with Susan, I knew I had found the right person to help me. I was at rock bottom and finally at the point you need to be, if you hope to succeed at therapy. I was prepared to do whatever the therapist told me to do to end my misery. I realized that a good therapist is worth their weight in gold when you find the one who is right for you. (I would tell anyone, in a heartbeat, to keep looking for as long as it takes to find the right one for you. You may have to go to several but don't give up and don't settle for less than you need to succeed.)

After my first visit with Susan I felt a thousand times better than I had in years. She began by telling me to let go of my past and to forgive myself...and I did. The part I liked the most about Susan is she gave me tools to use and homework to follow-up on every session. She is a student of the Jungian approach and she mined me into a student of Carl G. Jung, as well. I found it easy to buy into the theories he developed and shortly I was on my way to recovery. It worked for me very fast! The complete process took about a year with great effort on my part by following through on everything Susan taught me along with information I learned myself.

As soon as possible, I stopped the drugs Rachael put me on. I hated the drugs, because they dulled my senses and made me feel flat. (That is almost as bad as feeling depressed and then there were other side effects of the medication, too.) After about six months, I weaned myself off the drugs and continued therapy without it. (Rachael still doesn't believe I can live my life without the use of medication to control my negative thoughts but I thought she was wrong.) Eventually, her medical advice proved to be correct.

I worked on a new system of self-treatment for Depression and borrowed the idea from John Nash, Professor of Mathematics at Princeton University. (He was the topic of the movie, "A Beautiful Mind".) It took some time to work out a model that helped me overcome my depression but I did figure it out.

I owe a debt to all my angels for stepping in and offering the help I needed without judging me. People just don't know how to accept those with Mental Health disease. I believe it's out of fear that people believe it could happen to them. I can tell you from personal experience that having the world declare you insane or crazy is quite liberating for the person referred to as "The Nut". I no longer fear becoming crazy or insane because I'm already here and guess what: I survived. Now I'm even prospering.

The system that works for me involves the use of daily prayer along with maintaining a routine as much as possible. When I must deviate from a routine I am more aware to watch for signs of depression. I follow a rigid routine daily to avoid old pitfalls that used to make me feel like dirt under your shoe. Even with the methods I use to maintain the equilibrium I know I can fail at any time. I use that concern as motivation to stay hyper vigilant, not allowing myself to fall back into old habits. Additionally, one of the most important things I have learned in my on-going journey of self-discovery is that the easiest way to get through life is to *keep it simple.* Most of my life, I made things complicated, as human beings seem to have a propensity for doing when it really isn't necessary. I always recommend that people be truthful and candid, not only with others but also with themselves!

After my daily prayer, I tell myself how much I love me. Then I start the day with the same approach and attitude that I'm going to do good today in all endeavors. I always remember to be polite to every person or soul that I encounter each day. I never forget to be straightforward with people and leave no question in their mind about what I intend to do or express.

Finally, the most important step in my formula is to always remind myself that tomorrow offers possibilities, regardless of what has happened today or yesterday.

Along with a system of self-control over depression, there remains another very important element...my family! If not for my beautiful and intelligent wife who tolerated my acute depressive states and always supported me, I know I would have failed. I also have my bright, beautiful and talented daughter for whom I have constant feelings of pride and joy. She always makes me feel that I provide some essential purpose in her life and I take great satisfaction from this knowledge. The last but not least of my family support system is my Mother-in-law, Helen. I doubt she even knows how important she is to me, or how much I care about her. That is a situation I intend to correct now that she lives close enough for us to interact on a regular basis.

To all my Angels who taught me to take the time each day to look for angels all around us: You each played a part in saving my life and for that I am indebted. I now take the time to enjoy those little moments that we experience every day but are usually too busy or uptight to see. I stop to" smell the roses", if you will and continue to watch for angels. Someday I may be an angel for someone else in need!

Closing Comment

I hope you enjoyed reading this collection of stories I call my life. None of it would have been possible if not for one very courageous and unselfish woman who gave me life instead of terminating it. She certainly endured great hardship to do so following her brutal rape and life-threatening assault. Because I was allowed to live I know that I have positively impacted and perhaps saved lives. I had (and still have) a purpose for living...and my journey continues...thanks to Mercy.